# Back to Tuscany and the Barn

## By

## Catherine Carabine

# *Copyright:*

## Acknowledgements:

*To my husband Nick for his continued support, the countless hours of listening, reading, and for his undeniable amount of patience, thank you.*

*To my mum and dad for their encouragement and faith, and to all my good friends for their kind permissions allowing me to include and share moments from their lives.*

*A very big thank you to my friend Helen for all her help and time, who deserves at the very least a case of red wine from the Villa La Ripa estate, which I know she will thoroughly enjoy, Salute!*

*And lastly, I would like to acknowledge and remember Wayne Page, a man that is sadly missed by all......but one who will never be forgotten....*

For more about the 'Chestnut Barn'
visit www.achestnutbarnintuscany.com

# CHAPTER 1

The journey to England was one that was familiar,
and thankfully this time passed without mechanical
incident. Rover our Land Rover Freelander had in
fact conducted himself impeccably, contrary to his
usual behaviour. As I write I am prompted to 'touch
wood' for luck, or as the Italians do, *tocca di ferro,*
'touch iron' just in case I have spoken too soon. The
well-known landmark cities and towns were soon
behind us, together with the miles and passing hours.
My mood was subdued and pensive; I was
remembering all the wonderful moments Nick and I
had shared together often with new found friends.
Ironically the fatal 'pink sky' incident had made it all
possible, the unexpected event kept us there for
nearly a year; and my thoughts were tinged with an
overwhelming sense of relief as well as gratitude to
those who cared for Nick during those eighteen days
and nights and the critical forty eight hours that
could have changed my life forever.

Nick knowing me all too well had no need to ask
why I was so quiet. The tears that welled in my eyes

as I turned the keys on the large wrought iron grills that protected the doors and windows and left the Chestnut Barn, spoke volumes. He knew I was beyond consoling and for the moment remained silent.

The question had been asked on that final morning; although Nick, giving up his life in England and moving permanently to the Chestnut Barn, had given no immediate response; was perhaps a step too far. After finding out that I was half Italian; my passion for Italy came naturally, it was part of me, flowing through my veins; was it too much to ask?

I knew that for Nick the decision would not be taken lightly, there would be much deliberation and time for thought; I knew the process could not be rushed. My fear was that he would put it out of his mind entirely. The love for his sons and rapidly expanding number of grandchildren might be too powerful an influence. I had already done my 'soul searching' and I knew I could bear the parting. I would have Internet access so would be able to correspond with my parents daily if I wanted to. I would also be able to use the video link on my laptop.

Nick's boy's and their families were no strangers to the Chestnut Barn and I could see no reason why that should change. Yes we would be too far away for fleeting visits but we would be able to enjoy quality days together during the holidays. I hoped this might be enough to fill the months until Christmas each year when we would return. There's nothing quite like a Christmas spent with family.

Another hurdle to overcome was the small matter of our work commitments. There were too many questions and my mind was spinning.

On the ferry bound for Dover we were shrouded in drizzle and an impenetrable sea mist that seemed to mirror my very mood. On the bright side I would soon be seeing my parents and that thought raised my spirits. The question that was hanging in the balance could be left for another day....

Back in our daily work routine the weeks soon turned into months until one particularly bleak wet morning; the postman delivered one of Nick's many Independent Financial Adviser newspapers. This one flopped onto the mat like a wet sponge, the edges frayed, and the colour a deeper pink than usual, from the excessive amount of rainwater that it had absorbed in transit. After an hour on the radiator it resembled discarded fish and chip paper where in years past you might just make out a news story amongst the vinegar and grease while eating your supper. It was just about readable, not that Nick read them very frequently. I usually glanced through them first, highlighting any relevant articles that might be of interest to him and then found a use for them usually cleaning the smears off the windows or mirrors like the Victorians used to. Whether it was fate or plain boredom that set me on a rescue mission, I have no idea but I would like to believe it was fate. After carefully prising open the corner of each damp page and scanning the headlines an advertisement happened to catch my eye, it had been placed by an acquisitions agency they were looking for 'client banks', larger firms looking to buy in clients.

Nick had worked as a bank manager and latterly as an Independent Financial Adviser and had a number of clients that he looked after and advised. I say 'looked after' as Nick had known some of them for nearly twenty years and had been party to the usual lifetime events such as births, graduations, marriages, illnesses and unfortunately deaths. They were more than clients to Nick, they were friends; he would often do their banking, take some of them shopping or to the post office and on occasions even took the 'special few' out to lunch just to brighten their day and give them a change of scenery.

For some clients, relatives and friends were few and far between. The clients liked Nick immensely and his visits to their homes were often spent chatting casually over coffee and cakes; on some occasions 'pink gins' made an appearance! It was the favourite tipple of one of Nick's clients who was a gentleman in the true sense of the word, a Wing Commander and something of a celebrity; he had mixed with many famous people and loved to share his stories. His sister was a seamstress with Royal connections; he himself had been a pilot during the Second World War flying spies and resistance fighters into occupied France, landing and taking off under the cover of darkness. These were the stories that interested Nick with his penchant for history. Discussing investments and risk profiles was usually an afterthought. Nick cared, there was no 'sales pitch' or 'hard sell' if the client wanted to invest then he or she contacted Nick, he didn't need to go searching for introductions to new clients either, they came to him.

The 'pink sky' incident had made him take stock of his life and he had come to realise that it was all too fragile and could so easily be cut short without warning. Work had also become a little too tenuous and the Banking crisis had made clients more cautious; money was getting scarce.

The investment industry was precarious and the tightening of legislation was to thwart the less scrupulous advisers. This combined with the all too numerous changes in the regulations was hanging over the Financial Services Industry like the 'sword of Damocles'. Maybe this was the perfect time to think about reducing the personal stress that had become part of his life in more recent years.

A new generation of pseudo financial advisers in the form of client offspring were coming to the fore; their eyes firmly set on their inheritance they would do anything within their power to prevent their future capital from erosion. Even if it meant their aging mother or father going without much needed additional income 'You don't need the income mum....' Good advice given by Nick at the time of an investment could so easily turn into bad advice if it suited. The most trivial of complaints could easily turn into unwarranted fines imposed by the Financial Services Authority.

Client families that I had considered loving and caring were more often calculating, manipulative and devious; the rivalry between siblings frequently gave rise to misdeeds of unbelievable alacrity and cunning, especially when it came to inheritance. Compensation awards against professionally qualified advisers of integrity were snowballing out of all proportion. The Financial Services Authority regulators ruled in the plaintiffs favour more often than was defensible. This resulted in the indemnity insurance premiums becoming unreasonable. The first ten thousand pounds of any claim was the responsibility of the adviser and there was no right of appeal. The potential liability was staggering and the risks for the 'Independent Financial Adviser' were fast outstripping the rewards.

The in-depth form filling and report compilation, computerised risk assessment and 'money laundering' requirements even for fairly modest investments were beyond the comprehension of most clients. They even had to be told the extent of their life expectancy compared with the national average, an exercise few found favour with. Financial reports had to contain pie charts and graphs comparing risk with reward; soon they would need a PhD in mathematics to understand the complexities. To top it all if they were over a certain age they had to have the dreaded siblings present to sign to confirm that mum or dad was not too senile to take on board such new sciences.

The Managing Director of the company that licensed and monitored Nick's activities, if you like his 'umbrella company' was a man whose personal work philosophy was slog, slog and more slog. He spent more time than was healthy pursuing his own financial rewards, despite having a wife and two children at home. The window of his office was often still illuminated well into the evening, or alternatively he would be seen carrying a pile of files to his car to work on at home and even over a weekend. He collected 25% of the income generated by each of the advisers under his control and in return provided office support staff, stationery, compliance and a desk and telephone to the favoured few. Nick was not one of the favoured few and by necessity worked from home, with me as his administrator having gained my own professional qualifications. You might have thought that the 25% would be reduced in such circumstances, but no there were no concessions for the outsiders. People often said of him that he would secretly peel an orange in his pocket with one hand rather than having to share it!

Nick was expected to attend office meetings with all of his colleagues sat around the boardroom table listening to a diatribe of verbal diarrhoea that was supposed to educate, facilitate and indoctrinate, but it invariably left Nick drained of the will to live. The Managing Director was undeniably clever, but his training sessions took on the air of a small man (which he was) with small man syndrome desperately trying to demonstrate that he was cleverer than everyone present. It didn't take much persuading for Nick to agree to pursue the alternatives, even if he had to continue to work for the foreseeable future, working for another company was the better option.

It was some weeks before we were given the 'green light' and told that the sale of the 'client bank' was viable. Before we knew it we had steered another course and it was going to be a roller coaster of a ride. There in black and white posted on the Internet for all to see was an advertisement detailing Nick's business and sure enough as predicted by the Business Acquisition Company, the phone began to ring and emails flooded into our 'inbox'.

What we didn't know at the time was that the 'small man' was also looking to acquire 'client banks'. There would be a glut of retiring Independent Financial Advisers looking to leave the profession before the new legislation was imposed at the beginning of the New Year. The new regulations involved a string of additional qualifications and those of a certain age who resisted change in the firm belief that 'you shouldn't have to teach your grandmother to suck eggs' would also be seeking a way out. We just hoped that our 'small man' remained oblivious at least for the time being.

Meetings were arranged and more interest was shown than we had ever envisaged, we had companies from all over the South West vying for our attention and one company, some seventy miles away was paying particular interest. We were astonished, the 'small man' had always led us to believe rather dismissively that Nick's relatively small, but high net-worth client bank would attract no interest whatsoever. He had always claimed ownership of all clients under the 'company umbrella' and insisted that this was contractual, but we had never signed any such agreement. We had to be extremely careful that our covert operations remained undetected. Our biggest fear was that in this case the buyer and seller would somehow inadvertently be introduced and the proverbial you know what would 'hit the fan'.

The majority of the meetings went well and the choice was soon narrowed down to just two possibilities. Nick was keen to make sure that it would be the right move for his clients and indeed emphasised in negotiations, that he would be the one to undertake the client transfers and that he was to remain as a the first point of contact for them until a new client/adviser relationship had been established. Nick would remain as a Business Associate for an indefinite period. I was certain that Nick was going to relish the physical aspects of the transfer operation and I wish now that I had a pound for each time I heard the words 'transferred right from under his nose'.

We were certain that 'small man' would have done everything in his power to block our attempt, so Nick tirelessly began home visits across the county and beyond. Some of his contacts were as far away as Norfolk; he had one in Switzerland and two in France. The plan was starting to come together. Only four clients, who for logistical reasons declined to make the move; they would remain with 'small man' but had promised to remain silent; the rest willingly gave their support.

We had, more or less made a decision on the most suitable company. A beautiful Grade 1 listed, 4 Star

Elizabethan Country House Hotel was selected by mutual agreement for the final negotiations. Large French doors opened on to a neat and well-manicured formal garden, the lawn swept down to parkland, which lay beyond, and framed the typically English view across the rolling landscape. Judging from the well-suited clientele it was a popular choice amongst the business world. This was the perfect setting to make those all-important first impressions, and to cement new relationships. The food and wine were exquisite and the surroundings were as one might expect of a former stately home. In the elegance of the intimately sized dining hall amongst the silver cutlery, crystal wine goblets, crisp starched white tablecloths and fresh cut flowers my plan finally reached its conclusion

The final get together went extremely well, all three of us feeling at ease within minutes. The conversation continued long after the initial business discussions had been exhausted, and it was clear that a certain rapport had been established. The Principal Director was a qualified solicitor, the firm; previously part of a large legal practice was now an independent financial services company of undeniable quality. Our friendly negotiator was fully aware that we had already been approached with more than acceptable terms from other would be suitors, a vendors dream of course.

A deal was on the table together with an invitation to visit the company offices and meet the other two directors. With a lot to think about Nick spent the night and early hours of the morning in uneasy sleep, while I was imagining myself back at the Chestnut Barn working on the land during the day and snuggled up in front of the wood burners at night. I was almost there…

The following days continued to be a whirlwind of meetings, telephone calls and e-mails, a genuinely overwhelming experience. Nick finally agreed to go with the new company, as he felt sure they would provide a first class service to his client's.

Once all the legal issues were taken care of, we knuckled down to the administration side of things and letter upon letter was dispatched requesting the transfer of all financial investment agency business to the new company. The signed client transfer authorities were posted in one batch to the relevant investment companies and we sat back and waited for the 'you know what to hit the fan'.

Everyone seemed happy, the clients especially because they immediately received a far superior service from the new company; the directors were delighted and of course we were thrilled that everything proceeded without a hitch. Judging by the disgruntled and often savage e-mails we were receiving on the subject, the only person that wasn't happy was 'small man'. His personal e-mails contained words such as 'disingenuous' and the other more threatening terms, these I forwarded to our new company who had solicitors and barristers at their disposal. Having established that we were completely within our rights 'small man' resorted to a series of letters to Nick's clients, who merely added insult to injury by sending them all to Nick.

He responded by annotating each one with suitable wording and posting them back through the front door of 'small mans' offices. The settling of scores seemed complete. There were no fond farewells or parting handshakes amongst colleagues that Nick had once counted amongst his friends, they had turned away, for him the severance was poignant and final.

# CHAPTER 2

Looking back now it all seems like a lifetime ago, it was a move we should have considered years earlier, but it always seems easier to find a reason not to do something; a downturn in the housing market, can't sell the house, that fixed rate mortgage with the redemption penalty; a new wealthy client to get established, a credit card that needed paying off first. There are all sorts of seemingly more pressing reasons, all of them obstacles that you have to work your way through just to get to the starting line.

The barriers had finally been cast aside, fate and a wet newspaper had placed us on a path we were now going to give it a shot. We had nothing to loose and hopefully everything to gain - a stress-free lifestyle, a Mediterranean diet, healthcare that was second only to that of France in the 2000 World Health Organisation rankings, just a few of the positives. With our move would come the season's long dry hot summers the cool damp autumn that ran into December; the snow of February which would melt away in the spring warmth of March and April. A complete seasonal cycle! That is how it would be. 'Rose coloured spectacles' you might say and yes of course there would be negatives, but they would be different obstacles to overcome and we would laugh in the process or would we?

As the months passed, things began to slot into place; we were fortunate to agree the sale of our English home and there was enough money left over to tie up the loose ends. We packed up all our furniture and personal possessions, and then put some of them into storage to be sorted at a later date. Change of address letters were typed, signed and posted. Family members and close friends were notified of our imminent lifestyle change.

We would take some of our belongings with us to make the house feel like home and each time we visited England we planned to take a little more back with us. I carefully bubble-wrapped our favourite paintings and mementoes, boxed up some of our well-loved books and DVD's; followed by the more practical necessities such as clothing, laptops and all the essential personal documents that go with a lifetime of convention.

We bought and packed foodstuffs, which were either unobtainable in Italy or extortionately expensive. Items such as Porridge Oats were not only difficult to find but in Italy a 500g tin of white Quaker Oats is just under four euros the equivalent of £3.38, a far cry from the 1kg bags of Scottish Oats priced at around £1.20 in some of the major English supermarkets. Other items we decided to take were decaffeinated teabags, gravy granules, salad cream, horseradish, sage and onion stuffing, Marmite, Cheddar Cheese, black pudding, bacon and Cadburys Dairy Milk chocolate; all unobtainable where we were going. Although HP Sauce, Colman's Mustard, Heinz Baked Beans and Campbell's condensed tomato, and chicken soup, had made it onto the shelves. We would need off the shelf medicines like Paracetamol and Ibuprofen (both extremely expensive in Italy).

One of the larger must buys if you do not have a lot of space is a rotary washing line; I have never seen one in Italy. The common drying accessory is a *stendino* a foldaway metal or plastic framework strung with washing line supported by a very unstable set of crossover legs. They are certainly not well suited to the Tuscan summer winds that blow up the valleys without warning and can relegate the clean laundry to dirty washing in a matter of seconds.

Whilst on the subject of the garden, it seems impossible to buy an English style rectangular shaped garden spade. The many large owned large DIY stores and the older Italian family run ironmongers would stock a variety of heavy steel digging implements. The spade part is usually in the shape of what I can only describe as small medieval shield, at the end of a seven-foot pole. These are ideal tools for clearing the ditches, but pretty useless when trying to dig a straight line. For me, lifting the weight of it was just as difficult as digging the line. When the ground is hard the point of the spade sinks little more than a quarter of an inch and then proceeds to turn uncontrollably under the weight of your foot. Once you have completely lost your balance you tend to fall backwards which gives you just enough time to avoid the flailing pole before you land. The problem as I see it is that the sexes have far more clearly defined roles and the garden is the domain of the male; as a result the tools are entirely unsuitable for women to use.

Rover was now packed and ready to go, you would be forgiven for thinking that he was a mobile general store, loaded with just about everything you would need to set up home from scratch. We had packed the roof box with some of our most treasured possessions and lashed it to the roof bars with cargo straps as an extra precaution. All that was left to do was to say goodbye. My mum and I had both stated categorically that there would be no tears but the 'no crying' bit lasted for all of a minute; before my voice began to break and tears welled up in my eyes. My dad hugged me tightly and wished us both a safe journey; I continued to bite my bottom lip in a desperate attempt to keep it from quivering.

We had agreed that I would report our position on the road by e-mail at regular intervals along the route. My mum would monitor our progress using a map, which I had marked with a highlighter pen before leaving. I knew that she would find comfort in knowing where we were as we made our way through France and on into Italy. Having completed the journey with us on a previous occasion, she would be able to picture the scenery at the various chosen landmarks as we reached them.

We had planned to return to England during the month of May to sort out one or two work related issues and it would only be a matter of weeks before we would have to return. On this occasion Rover would be spared the arduous journey as we would fly by lost cost airline and hire a small car to travel from London Stansted Airport, to Devon.

So here we were, loaded to the gunnels and as the wheels turned for those first few yards of the one thousand two hundred miles we were about to cover, I was filled with the mixed emotions of apprehension, sadness and excitement. I was now desperately trying to regain some composure and whilst waving goodbye I had to place my hand in front of my face to hide the floods of tears that came. Soon we were on our way to Dover and the ferry terminal and that narrow strip of ocean that separated us from our old life. The culmination of months of planning had finally been reached and I had let go.

The white cliffs gradually faded into the distance, lost in the sea mist that engulfed them, the seventy-minute ferry trip passed almost too quickly and we were on foreign soil. The thought came to me that neither of us could speak either French or Italian particularly well and we were now entirely at the mercy of our European neighbours; whom had not always looked upon the English with favour. It was always going to be a challenge but we were both ready for whatever lay ahead.

The French motorways always seemed to carry very little traffic and we soon made good progress heading south towards the Monte Blanc tunnel that would take us across the border and into Italy. Arriving in darkness and the beginnings of a snowstorm we stopped overnight in our regular hotel in the foothills of the Alps on the French side. Dinner in comfortable surroundings was followed by an early night and while we slept soundly the snow drifted silently down leaving a blanket of white to greet us in the dim light of the early morning. The car park lay several centimetres deep in snow, but the black lines of cleared roads cut a path south towards an Italian spring. The sun, rising above the towering mountains cast a golden sheen across the white landscape as devoted skiers and boarders poured from the pretty wooden chalets eager to be the first to carve their lines through the freshly fallen snow.

The Aosta valley dotted with castles, monasteries and long abandoned hamlets is the first and one of the most beautiful sights that greets you as you leave the darkness of the tunnel and pass into Italy; for me it is always a highlight of the journey. I have seen the splendour of it in spring, summer, autumn and winter and it never ceases to make my heart skip a beat.

Hours of motorway driving soon passed and before we knew it we were within an hour of our *Autostrada* exit from where we would take the minor roads to our home. We had covered more than one thousand miles without incident, but now we ran into a traffic jam that stretched as far as the eye could see, and rather ominously there was no traffic coming towards us on the north bound carriageway; it was clear that there had been a major incident. We had come to a halt and there was no way of getting off the main road. Italian drivers and passengers were out of their cars milling around and trying to find out from fellow travellers what was causing the hold up. Loud music boomed from what I can only describe as a 'cute' Fiat Cinquecento just a few cars in front and its female passengers danced unashamedly on the tarmac. Others were busy either texting or talking on their mobile telephones, an activity which most Italians seem to be obsessed with, even when driving. As in England the use of a telephone whilst at the wheel is totally prohibited by Italian law but that never seems to deter them. I have even encountered drivers on the wrong side of the road coming towards me, telephones pressed to their ears and offering an apologetic wave as they narrowly avoid slicing off the front wing of the car. Something that was noticeable by its absence however, was any expression of frustration or rage, in fact an almost carnival atmosphere prevailed over the whole scene; none of us were going anywhere so we might as well all just relax.

We were there for sometime before the screams of sirens passed on the hard shoulder to our right; first the *Carabinieri* (military police) then the *Polizia de Stato* (state police) then the *Polizia Stradale* (traffic police) and finally the *Corpo Forestale* (forest rangers) who also seem to have some authority where traffic incidents are concerned, either that or they were late for their tea who knows; officers of the law are very much a mystery to Nick and I, as you will find out later. Slowly we began to creep forward and on turning a bend, there ahead of us was a scene of utter devastation. A car transporter had hit the central reservation and jettisoned its load of at least ten brand new cars onto both carriageways. Oncoming vehicles had obviously collided with them; crushed metal, glass and other debris lay scattered in all directions. Ambulances, fire engines and tow trucks littered the narrow inside lane where officials were all frantically going about their business trying to deal with the crisis as efficiently as possible. Fortunately there seemed to be very few casualties.

Two hours passed and we were once again on the move, heading up the *Passo dello Spino* the SS208 that snakes it way upwards to an altitude of over one thousand metres from the town of Pieve San Stefano towards Chuisi della Verna. It is a road full of sharp hairpins, where one of the most popular Tuscan hill-climb races is staged annually in June. The first car race took place back in September 1965 when eighty- six competitors participated, the following year it played centre stage to the *Giro Automobilistico d'Italia*, many more famous races followed as well as the Motorbike races. It has a huge following and even in the late sixties drew crowds of over forty thousand people. The road is well known today amongst racing drivers and motorbike riders alike as a natural mountain racetrack. Travelling it is all very well if you happen to be the driver, for me however it is a road that provokes an overwhelming feeling of motion sickness, no matter how hard I try to focus on the road. Sadly many people have been killed in accidents on this road, bunches of flowers and perpetual candles pay tribute to the victim's it has claimed over the years, one of which we even had the misfortune to witness, a horror that both Nick and I will never forget. It was a motorcyclist, he had obviously misjudged the bend, hit the crash barrier and been thrown over the side, sadly the young man died and we heard later that he had left behind a wife who was expecting their first baby. We pass this spot quite frequently and every time we do we spare a thought for the mother, and the child who will never know its father.

As we entered the little village of Lama, which lies below Fragaiolo there was a hive of activity; some of the residents were casually sweeping their doorsteps, whilst others were just simply chatting and soaking up the warmth of the March sunshine. The small corner shop was bustling with activity both inside and out. An array of plant trays cluttering the pavement seemed to be the centre of attention as some of the local men rummaged through them seeking the strongest and most healthy vegetable seedlings. The plants were soon to be re-homed and lovingly cared for in nearby *orti* or vegetable gardens. As we passed slowly through, smiles, nods and waves greeted us, the familiar sight of the old man, leaning on his stick whilst sat on the bench outside the shop, dressed in a white shirt and trousers with braces, his head topped off with a cap. It was as if we hadn't been away, everything still as it was and it felt good to be recognised and once again part of a community.

As we left the village behind the familiar track that scaled the heights to the Chestnut Barn came into view, it was in a sorry state of repair, the torrents of winter rain and melted snow having carved channels into the gravel and soil, but thankfully it was nothing Rover our faithful and by now ageing Land Rover couldn't cope with. Snow still clung to the mountain opposite and traces remained in pockets in the shadows of the woodland out of reach of the suns rays. The landscape that was emerging from the winter snow looked almost barren. We had learnt that the autumnal brown clusters of dead leaves that clung to the tree would remain in place until the new life pushed them away, unyielding despite the force of the winds that often swept down the mountain. The grassed areas were yellow, singed by the extreme cold, the brambles looked crushed and lifeless, and the Spanish Broom or *ginestra* carried traces of snow on the tips of their tendrils like they had been dipped in white paint. Old Man's Beard was trying to smother some of the small chestnuts trees that we had tried to encourage during our previous time here, its white feathery flowers stood out against the dark boughs that had been stripped of life during our absence. The first signs of leaf buds on the branches told us that all was not lost, each tree in turn cried out to be rescued from the stranglehold that had established itself with menacing haste. We would come to discover in time that the warmth of the spring sunshine would bring the welcome and the unwelcome in almost equal measure.

Our bodies needed a little time to adjust from the constant motion that we had endured over the last twenty or so hours, so we would leave the unpacking at least for another day. We wandered aimlessly around the garden taking in all the familiar sights as well as the new. Much had changed brambles had reclaimed some of the land, one or two of the old pines on the lower terraces which had once been adorned with immaculately manicured chestnut trees, had fallen in the gales of December and January. Fortunately none were within reach of the Chestnut Barn, but it was a reminder that nothing on this mountain should be left to chance. Small fragments of terracotta roof, *tegola* lay on the stone terrace and crunched under our feet. As we continued our inspection we noticed that a good few of the tiles on each of the four roofs would need replacing during the coming weeks.

The snow and frost of February had inevitably taken its toll on the outside and with keys in hand we approached the large grills that protected the patio doors with trepidation. The metal doors inside the grills opened noisily as we peered through the gap but all seemed in order apart from the odd dead scorpion that could not cope with the winter chill and other strange looking insects that must have sought shelter and died as the summer turned to autumn and winter. With a few flips of switches inside the fuse box, life returned to the Chestnut Barn, crystal clear water spluttered through the taps and from the showerhead. The fridge purred into action and soon the place began to feel like a home again.

The two wood-burners were the only source of heating, apart from a low powered electric fire and one of those small halogen heaters that manages to heat no more than a few cubic feet near the ground and which never seems to penetrate the thickness of your slippers. October in Italy is generally very warm during the day, but the nights can be contrastingly cold and the cutting of wood for the burners during our visit then, had seemed to dictate our every movement. The Internet had provided a very detailed weather report for periods of three days so we would cut as much of the wood that had been left behind from the last coppicing as we could manage. The result of these labours produced what seemed an endless supply of cut logs and kindling, there was nothing more to do now than light the wood burners. We retrieved the necessary essentials from Rover and settled down for the afternoon with the thought of maybe relaxing with a book, and once again, time became of little importance.

# CHAPTER 3

Suitably refreshed after a long sleep that extended well into the morning we made a start on unpacking, one by one our treasured pictures were unwrapped and positioned on the cream coloured walls. The chestnut wood and glass display cabinet we had purchased the year before was tastefully filled with some of our favourite possessions; the rest would have to wait for another year or until the next trip in Rover. The bookcases were packed to the gills with Nick's much loved and well thumbed history books. Items of clothing hung on hangers in the large solid chestnut wardrobes and the remainder neatly packed away in the matching chests of draws. The Barn was beginning to feel homely.

There is an endless supply of chestnut wood in this region of Tuscany due to the vast number of groves which remain and are still tended by sons and grandsons, but as the generations have passed away an even larger number have sadly been felled and subsequently been turned into furniture. Chestnuts were, and still are a source of food eaten whole, made into pastes, creams, and alcohol or dried and ground to make flour, for bread and cakes. Two annual festivals solely dedicated to the chestnuts or *castagne* are held on consecutive weekends during October, in Caprese Michelangelo. The festivals attract thousands of visitors from far and wide all eager to sample the chestnut based delicacies.

That afternoon dark clouds appeared from nowhere, darkening the landscape they sat unmoving, ominously shrouding the ridge of Monte il Castello, the mountain that rises for another five hundred metres above the Barn. Suddenly, a flash of lightening turned the hillside into a mass of colour and the sound of thunder resounded through the valley below. The skies opened, a sound like an approaching express train came down the hillside heading towards the Barn whilst hailstones the size of marbles struck the ground. The storm continued unabated for the next fifteen minutes, the hailstones bounced off the metal garden table and chairs, the noise was deafening; by the time it had finished there was a carpet of white ice as far as the eye could see. The roof of the Land Rover was peppered with tiny indentations. Two hours later the clouds had passed, the warmth from the sun was approaching twenty-five degrees Celsius, the winter carpet had gone and a clean earthy smell swept through the forest on a warm, gentle breeze. There was always something astonishing and mystifying happening; every dawn that came brought similar new experiences to delight the senses.

In the days that followed there was more rain, so we were confined to the Barn; we were grateful that we had had Internet access installed. The system bounced signals into the Barn from the little town of Caprese Michelangelo. Leaving the antenna, situated on the school building the signal came up the mountainside and was picked up by our receiver at the top of the long scaffolding pole that Nick had erected on our last visit. A series of high-tension cables transferred the transmission via a Wi-Fi box to another electronic pad, which in turn transferred it to the Barn. You may think that I am easily pleased but I am totally amazed at what technology can provide. We could keep in contact with our families and clients, watch BBC television and still feel part of the outside world.

One hot topic that was big news, not just here in Italy, but for the 1.2 billion Catholics all over the world was the news that Pope Benedict XVI had formally resigned. It had been announced on the 28th February 2013 and was said to be due to his failing health. It was today, Tuesday 12th March, that the Papal Conclave was convened to begin the process of electing the new Pope. Conclave comes from the Latin *cum clavis* meaning with key. Pope Benedict XVI was the first Pope to relinquish the office since Pope Gregory XII in 1415. Now, one hundred and fifteen Cardinals from all over the world would be locked into the Sistine chapel until a new pope was elected... This tradition dates back to 1274 when Pope Gregory X decreed, that electors should be locked in seclusion to prevent the political interference and long vacancies between Popes that had become a norm. In fact, since 2005 the cardinals do not remain under lock and key in the Sistine chapel but remain in the confines of Vatican City with no access to newspapers, television, radio, Internet or telephones for the duration of the process. In the past century no Conclave has lasted more than five days, most ending within two or three.

News coverage was unbroken with many Internet sites showing live pictures of the all important chimney, where at 7.42pm in Rome the awaiting crowd of over 100,000, sighed as black smoke rose and cries of *fumata nera* could be heard; the vote was inconclusive. Whilst the TV channels all vied to break the news first, they and I would have to be patient and wait another night.

Day two, again I followed the proceedings with interest much to Nick's dismay. Being a Catholic, admittedly not a practising one, in my own mind I thought I could at least partially redeem myself by continuing to watch. Nick left me to it and continued with his research relating to the First World War. All eyes were again upon St Peters Square, the crowds had grown and the tension was mounting. At 11.40am the result was again the same, black smoke, inconclusive. In October 1958 grey smoked was produced and caused much confusion not only once but twice, since 2005 the bells of St Peters Basilica are also rung to avoid any confusion.

Later that evening at 7.07pm all eyes were once more upon the chimney and this time came the cries *fumata bianca*, white smoke billowed from the chimney and the bells of St Peters resonated around that unmistakably famous square. The crowds' cheers of jubilation, together with the waving of flags of all nationalities and banners with the words *Viva il Papa*, made it quite a spectacle. Members of the Catholic faith were happy, and now all that remained was to see which Cardinal had been chosen. After lengthy speculation from the various news teams, the cameras became firmly fixed on the balcony overlooking the Square. At 8.25pm the curtain fluttered behind the deep scarlet drapes the most senior cardinal stepped forward and announced *Habemus Papam*, we have a new Pope. The 266th Pope was Cardinal Jorge Mario Bergoglio, a Jesuit, aged 76 from Argentina, his chosen name, 'Pope Francis'.

The new Pope also becomes Head of State for the Vatican City. The Vatican has a population of 831; most of the residents are priests and nuns; twenty-two of the Vatican's residents are children, offspring to the 110 Swiss Guards that live tucked away behind St Peters Square with their families. The guarding of the Pope began in 1506 when the reigning Pope recruited mercenaries from Switzerland for protection. The guards are unmistakable, dressed in their yellow, blue, red and white uniforms holding aloft halberds. Some say Michelangelo designed the tunics; however the current uniform was fashioned in 1914 by Jules Repond, each tunic custom made for each guard and made up of 154 pieces of fabric. Finally a nametag is pinned to the finished garment to avoid confusion in the changing rooms near the armoury.

After having been subjected to more than his fair share of Papal and religious news Nick, being more of a conspiracy theorist than a religious follower, needed a change of scenery. Deciding to reacquaint ourselves with the surrounding countryside we took a stroll towards the ford that crosses the river at the bottom of the valley and if our stamina prevailed, we would ascend the mountain beyond, towards the peaks of Monte il Castello.

The woods and chestnut groves were much the same as when we had last seen them apart from a few small parcels of land which had been cleared of three, out every four trees, the boughs and trunks now lay carefully stacked in metre lengths near the track ready for collection. Even the twigs had been cut into lengths, bound with string, and stacked into neat piles ready for use as kindling. Nothing is wasted!

The woodmen could stand on slopes more acute than forty-five degrees and still keep their grip on a slippery surface of fallen leaves and soft compost, whilst at the same time brandishing a heavy chainsaw like it was no more than an electric carving knife. They move like mountain goats on narrow paths bringing trees down like corn in the wake of a scythe. In times gone by donkeys would pull carts up into the hills to retrieve the cut wood and kindling and sell it door to door in the local towns and villages. Nowadays large articulated lorries and tractors with deep trailers trundle up the track at regular intervals taking the wood away in bulk to the factories where it is cut into usable planks; the saw dust is used to make pellets for the *stufa a pellet,* room heaters and central heating boilers that are starting to replace the traditional wood-burners.

The ford was in full flood after the considerable amount of rain and snow that the area had suffered over the last six weeks. The snow had apparently fallen right on cue at the end of January and continued without any respite until the end of February. The ground was now soaked and the surface water struggled to drain away. Where the snow had drifted in deep pockets in the hillsides the prints of deer, porcupine and boar were everywhere, we wondered how they possibly could have survived. One such print caught our attention as it appeared to have been made by a large dog or cat, so large in fact that I took a picture of it on my mobile phone. It may have been larger than when it was created because of the melting snow, although I was not entirely convinced so I put it to the back of my mind for now.

We had learnt that power lines had been down and many of the small hamlets had intermittently been without electricity. Oil lamps, bottled gas-stoves and heaters were the only means of light, warmth and cooking. Fortunately, most people had wood burners but those who had moved towards the more modern pellet stoves found them of no use during power cuts, as electricity is needed to ignite the combustion chamber and drive the fan.

As the seasons are more clearly defined at the Chestnut Barn it would be a much easier task to prepare for the worst that the weather could throw at us. We are approximately one thousand metres above sea level and would always be subjected to the extremes. It would be important to stockpile certain items of food to keep us going when we were cut off, so a small chest freezer was high on my list of items to acquire. After our last unforgettable experiences trying to get the shopping up the track in two feet of snow with only the aid of a plastic baby bath, I was determined to be better prepared; but for now, winter was a long way off.

The forces of nature struck again during the night, the clear powder-blue skies of the afternoon clouded over towards dusk and until the following morning torrential rain swept the mountain as if trying to hose away the last remnants of winter. The sound against the roof tiles kept us from restful sleep and stayed with us until well into the following night. The pockets of snow that lay on Monte il Castello had at last been reduced to water. Logs in the bucket near the fire were rapidly being used and I knew the time was fast approaching for Nick to brave the unrelenting storm and venture out as far as 'The Alamo' our self built log cabin/wood store. So out he went dressed in a

waxed jacket, matching hat, waterproof trousers tucked into his Wellington boots that came half way up his legs. I went only as far as the *loggia* where I stood listening and watching, as the rain surged over the edge of the roof tiles onto the paving under my feet. It was as if we were in the middle of a tropical storm, the volume of water falling from the sky was incessant, beyond imagination, and there was no sign of it abating!

Nick now back under the shelter of the *loggia,* put down the laden wood buckets, picked up a shovel and headed back towards 'The Alamo'. He said something in passing, but the noise was so tremendous that I heard none of his words, but he seemed to be in a hurry. I dashed inside and threw on my waterproofs and Wellingtons and ran after him.

The water flooded down from the banks at the front of the Chestnut Barn and a river two to three inches deep flowed past the front door, down the gravel path towards 'The Alamo' and the shed where all of the garden equipment and power tools were stored. The shed looked like it was about to be carried away towards Valboncione the village several hundred feet below. Nick was frantically digging a channel trying to divert the water away from both buildings. I grabbed a garden hoe and began to scrape gullies in the gravel drive on the level above, creating a series of small dams and channels. Within a matter of minutes we were both drenched, looking like a pair of drowned rats.

We had succeeded in saving the shed but the water had cut another path down the 'white road' that came up to the Barn from the *comune* road below. This stretch is about two hundred metres in length; we had spent large sums of money adding a grey, almost black gravel mixture of various grades, and had bedded down nicely to form a relatively smooth

33

surface. It was now looking more like the Nile Delta than anything approaching a road; half way down it a massive spout of water was shooting two feet into the air. Off we went armed with our shovel and hoe looking like Don Quixote and Sancho without the horse and donkey, to investigate. The bank on the left hand side had collapsed and blocked the deep gully we had dug the previous year to take the water away from the road. The spout was a result of the fast flowing water hitting the blocked entrance to a large bore pipe that passed under the road, through the lower wood, before entering the *comune* drain and eventually on to the river, deep in the valley. The water from the spout had practically washed away a stretch of road of at least ten metres in length; all that remained were some very large boulders, which were too heavy to succumb. We were left with a stretch that even Rover would struggle to pass over. To top it all, the water had undermined the roots of a massive tree that was over one hundred feet in height; its trunk alone must have been four metres in diameter it now lay forlornly sprawled across some land that we didn't own. Fortunately the land had never been tended to for as long as we had been around so it was not going to be high on our list of jobs to be done. The immediate concern was clearing the entrance to the large bore pipe, and after three hours of continuous digging we were able to return to the warmth and shelter of the Chestnut Barn.

The road would be made good with a lorry load of the grey gravel and a few days of back breaking raking and shovelling. For now though it would have to wait until the weather improved, and the spring downpours were well and truly over. In the meantime it would put Rover through his paces on several occasions and test his off road capabilities virtually to the limit.

The first test would come all too soon, in need of more milk we headed down to the village of Lama, as our own village shop in Fragaiolo was closed. On a previous occasion and on a wine buying foray I had spotted a rather nice bottle of *Brunello* marked up at the extraordinarily cheap price of nine euros, I would normally expect to pay anything upwards of twenty euros in a supermarket and in restaurants it is priced anything from forty to one hundred euros depending on the year. I hasten to add, far and above anything we would normally buy. This is Italy's premier wine; a well-known and highly revered, fine full bodied red wine from the Montalcino region of Tuscany. I checked again and sure enough the fluorescent orange price label read nine euros. Rather guiltily I approached the till expecting to be told that the price was a mistake and having to embarrassingly hand the bottle back. It was a tense moment as I sheepishly returned to Rover, bottle in hand anticipating a tap on the shoulder at any moment. After seeing the expression on my face Nick's first words were "Go on, what's happened now?"

"Just drive." I said without further explanation feeling like I had just robbed a post office. I did eventually explain, Nick was all for returning to see if there were any more but I had visions of him rummaging through the shelves like the first day of the after Christmas sales and my sin would undoubtedly be found out. Now every time I enter the shop I do so with trepidation and I look at the shop assistant as if she must be thinking 'Ah yes, I remember you from the *Brunello* incident', I imagine her proceeding to check each item I have gathered, against a price list, looking up through squinting eyes and frowning at me with a questioning look, the colour rising in my guilty cheeks. A few years have passed since that day and there is little I can do to stop Nick accompanying me on every visit even if I only need a pint of milk. He stands there furtively examining the wine shelves head rising and falling in an endeavour to look between the lines of the neatly placed bottles. Unfortunately or from my point of view fortunately, he has never come across another mis-priced bottle of *Brunello*. I don't think I could go through the anxiety again.

*

With my single carton of milk in hand, Nick and I hurried out of the door and across the road to Rover, the rain still bucketing down and showing no sign of letting up. Having moved off at the first bend we encountered a very old open-cab tractor, moving sluggishly up the hill, it looked as if it should be in an agricultural museum. A cloud of exhaust was escaping its rear end and vanishing in great swirls into the rain. The driver was holding aloft a bright pink coloured umbrella in his right hand whilst his left hand and his right knee he was carefully trying to persuade the steering wheel to help the wheels negotiate the fast approaching hairpin bend. A change of gear was totally impractical so his speed was reduced to a crawl. The driver was unaware of our presence and I don't think it would have mattered if he had known we were there. Rover, already reduced to plodding along in first gear struggled to avoid stalling and was only able to proceed with liberal use of the clutch. A simultaneous shake of the head, laughter and the words, 'Well this *is* Italy' followed; it seemed that nothing could surprise us now.

As the months passed we would begin to find out that there are two items that regularly need replacing on cars, the clutch is one and the tyres are the other; the hairpin bends, tractors and hills take their toll but come with the territory. The other thing to remember if you visit or move to Italy is that during the winter month's snow tyres must be fitted or snow chains carried from November through to April, these dates many vary according to your province.

Further along the road we came across an English neighbour called Wayne, who with his wife Pamela and an extremely sociable and affectionate Irish Setter named Rufus, had set up home two years ago in the former priests house in the small hamlet below Fragaiolo called Colle di Fragaiolo. They were someway ahead of us in the learning curve of surviving in a new country and although it was good to try and integrate into the Italian community it was reassuring to know we had nice English speaking neighbours close by, that we could turn to for advice or help if we needed it.

They had told us an unsettling story of an occasion during the winter months when they had seen from the window of their house, what they described as a 'big cat' traversing the fields behind the house; it was easily recognisable by the long and lean upturned, curved tail. Our *geometra* or architect had spoken of 'mountain lions' during one of his visits to the Barn, but we had always suspected that something may have been lost in translation or we had misheard. Now we had confirmation of the existence of such animals; my thoughts instantly returned to the footprint we had found in the forest and I wondered if the large cat had decided to venture higher up the mountain in search of food. At the time I thought no more about it until later, when out walking the same print appeared in soft mud just above the Chestnut Barn. There was no question of any distortion as a result of melting snow now; it looked far too large to be that of a hunting dog. In any case the hunting season was over and young boar and deer were appearing in large numbers. I had taken photos of the footprint or *orma*, in conjunction with my mobile phone case to give some idea of the proportions. When shopping in the village I showed them to some of the villagers who had gathered for coffee, after much discussion, gesticulating, the shaking and nodding of heads, the verdict was unanimous, we had a wolf!

In England wolves had been extinct since the reign of King Henry VII between the late 1400s and early 1500s, so the existence of wolves in the forests around the Barn gave immediate cause for concern, although the locals seemed totally unphased.

'*Sì, sì un lupo*', was all I could glean from the gathering along with a smile, then the conversation quickly turned to something more interesting. The smiles seemed almost sympathetic as though I was being neurotic and beyond help. Once at home we immediately consulted the Internet searching various sites for final affirmation, and there, in black and white were a number of interesting links, many written by reputable academics. The information provided detailed statistics, behavioural habits and more importantly as far as I was concerned, various geographic locations. Wolves have lived in Tuscany and the Apennines for centuries living off a diet that normally consisted of wild boar or *cinghiale,* closely followed by *daino* – fallow deer or *capriole* - roe deer. The article also mentioned that a small number of attacks had been made on livestock and pets although very rarely. Particular reference was made to large numbers living in the forests in the Arezzo area, the city separated from the Barn by no more than twenty kilometres as the crow flies. The densely forested hills that climb up to the peaks of Monte il Castello, Monte Altuccia and the Regina Ridge where we lived, was the home to freely roaming wolves.

I went on to find out that these wolves did not tend to hunt in packs; they were solitary predators, usually very shy and much more afraid of me than I was of them. Their mating period being mid-March, with a gestation period of only 2 months, a female can produce 2-8 pups. They are normally a blended dark brown or grey colour, although black specimens have also been sighted. In 1984 they became a protected species; unfortunately however some are still killed through random poisonings and road accidents. When the weather is particularly severe the wolves tend to scavenge around human habitations becoming desperate for food. A male wolf can average in weight from 24-40 kilograms and has a body length of usually 100-140cm. The wolf has always been a big part of the Italian National Identity. Mystery and legend would have it that a she-wolf raised the founders of Rome, Romulus and Remus.

Gubbio, which is a beautiful medieval town situated approximately ninety kilometres south east of the Barn, is also famous for its legend of a wolf, dating from the year 1206. Saint Francis of Assisi had discovered that a wolf had been terrorising the townsfolk by killing, not only animal stocks but also the farmers, whilst they were trying to protect them.

St. Francis set out into the forest to find the wolf. According to the book 'Little Flowers of St Francis' people upon hearing this pleaded with him not to go, but undeterred he continued on his quest. Soon he came across the wolf, its hackles raised and teeth bared; the wolf began to approach Saint Francis who managed to stop the wolf in mid stride by forming the sign of the cross with his arms. He then ordered 'Brother Wolf' to come to him and lay down at his feet. After reprimanding the wolf for his bad behaviour Francis is said to have bargained with the wolf. The wolf and St Francis eventually agreed that the wolf would end his spate of killing but only if the people of Gubbio gave him food everyday, this pact was sealed by the raising of his paw to the hand of St Francis. Together they returned to the town where a large gathering had formed in the *piazza* and St Francis began to preach from a rock which is now enshrined in the church of San Francesco. It was on this spot that the town's people agreed to the proposal and the wolf immediately agreed to end his reign of terror. The wolf died two years later and during excavations that took place in the 19th century; archaeologists unearthed the skeleton of the wolf that the townspeople had enshrined there.

Many months have passed since we first discovered the existence of our nocturnal canine visitor but to this day we have not had rare privilege of seeing our *lupo.*

# CHAPTER 4

Cutting wood for the burners was now down to a fine art, almost mechanical in its execution. I loaded the blue metal saw horse with previously cut lengths and moved them along the length of the horse until the last log fell to the ground. It was like a well-oiled production line. Nick used the chainsaw to cut the timber into the right size to fit inside the burners. He would then split the thicker logs with a large and very sharp axe usually into two or four pieces depending on the thickness. The noise of the dry logs falling from the chopping block reminded me of school music lessons; the sound of a hammer striking a glockenspiel.

We had learnt from previous experiences and from reading articles on the Internet that some species of tree gave off toxic fumes when burnt, and that if the sawdust and smoke was inhaled it could be harmful. Chestnut would not give off dangerous fumes when burnt but we had noticed that inhaling the dust gave rise to sore throats, headaches and often swollen glands in the neck which lasted for two or three days. To prevent this we wore white facemasks the sort you would use when decorating or sanding wood. With his ear defenders, hard-hat and mask I couldn't help but compare Nick's facial appearance to that of a Duck Billed Platypus and these regular wood cutting sorties always brought a hidden smile to my lips. My eyes gave the game away and he would say, 'You're laughing at me.' and more often than not I was reduced to tears and uncontrollable laughter, although I never mentioned the word Platypus. It was hard work though and the exercise left us both with aches and pains in places you wouldn't imagine. Over time we began to lose a few pounds and started to tighten up and tone those previously little used muscles.

As mundane as these necessary work interludes might seem there was always something to wonder at during those hours spent in the forest. Most of the logs we were cutting up were taken from the dead chestnut trees and when you cut into them you were never quite sure of what you were going to find. Apparently there is a European 'Red List' of endangered species of 'Saproxylic' beetles; these beetles depend entirely on decaying wood to survive. One such creature appeared on one of our forest excursions, the likes of which was beyond imagination. What emerged from a large hole bored deep into one trunk of decaying chestnut was a creature I have since discovered is called 'Cerambix Miles'. Its body is three inches in length and its skin armoured rather like that of a hippopotamus. From its head protrudes two thin antennae, both of which are almost three times its body length when fully extended. When inside the hole in the trunk these antennae are folded back along each side of the body. The body itself appears to be in three sections and it moves on six legs at an incredibly slow pace, the antennae waving about as it does so. Stag beetles are another now extremely rare species, which we often encounter in the forest at certain times of the year. On one occasion we came across a colony of what looked suspiciously like death watch beetle, small round black creatures like large ladybirds that would certainly be unwelcome guests in the Chestnut Barn's heavy chestnut beams. They can bore deep into the wood, carving out huge chambers that eventually cause the beams to collapse. We once discovered one hastily making its way from the log bucket up the wall towards the ceiling; luckily Nick caught it in time and sent it packing. Now we never leave the log buckets in the house when we are not there to keep an eye on them; you just never know what's lurking about.

A friend who bought a house nearby to renovate, decided that he wanted to leave some of the old beams and window lintels in place to add character to the house. In the silence of the night he could hear what he thought were munching noises coming from deep within the wood. Experts later told him that it was the beetles mating call and that he would be wise to have the sections treated before whatever it was found a mate!

Sometimes inside the thicker tree trunks we encounter beautifully constructed cells and tiny chambers all linked together by tunnels. The cells are usually packed with wood ants, the largest of all the ant species we have seen. In the winter months and in early spring they appear drowsy and still in hibernation, but in the heat of the summer they move rapidly like Army Ants in the Amazon Rain Forest. They are black and about one centimetre in length and if they take a fancy to your beautifully constructed chestnut fences you could be left with a pile of sawdust in no time at all.

We are now learning as much as we can about the habitat we share with so many beautiful creatures and have embarked upon educating ourselves into ways of preserving and encouraging their development. Bird and bat boxes have been strategically placed in positions of shade to ensure successful breeding, but not too far away to stop us from enjoying their comings and goings. It must be said that not all creatures are so welcome in and around the Barn, but I will leave this topic until the sun really comes out.

*

After establishing a large stack of firewood and cleaning ourselves up a bit, we took a trip down to the local shop to see if the post lady had left any mail for us. When living in a fairly remote location the village shop comes into its own. It is one of those places where people congregate, a fountain of local knowledge and a hub of communication that needs to be regularly plundered to best advantage. As always Tatianna a local girl who runs the shop warmly greeted us. Tatianna had very kindly agreed to keep our mail, our track still suffering with the scars of winter and not currently passable to Elsabetta, the post lady's Fiat Panda. The shop was the heart of the community. During the warmer weather even when closed the older men occupy the red plastic table and chairs left out by their absent host and play cards or just chat.

Public notices are often displayed on a board outside the shop and it is here that the Italian Electricity company ENEL would post warnings of intended repairs to electricity lines when the supply would be interrupted, sometimes for several hours during the day. Further up the mountain towards the hamlet of Valboncione the advices would be pasted to the large refuge and recycling bins that are found at regular intervals along the road; there is no door-to-door collection anywhere in Italy. There is a blue bin for plastic, green/silver for food waste, yellow for cardboard and green for glass. Larger objects or metal are simply left by the side and collected at the same time. It is a system that seems to work well, considering the logistics of getting to isolated villas and farms.

Valboncione was the end of the line as far as the tarmac road went and only has six permanent residents out of a possible twenty-seven, the others having moved away to the cities and coastal resorts to find work. Some return in the height of summer usually during August when most of the rest of Italy seems to shut down. The windows and doors of the old houses are then left shuttered and barred for the rest of the year. The existence of the last six mainly elderly residents is represented by the occasional bark of a dog, a wisp of smoke rising from a chimney pot or the distant chattering of an Italian television set. In the silence of the siesta a peaceful tranquillity settles over the landscape.

When living in this part of Tuscany it is as well to remember that not everything goes according to plan and there is much that I can look back on that I took for granted when living in England. Shopping is one example, in Italy unlike England most shops are closed on Sundays and the only emergency foods available are from filling stations usually situated on the main highways. During the summer months the Spar shop situated in Lama will open but it is a devil of a job to remember exactly when the service begins and ends, let alone the hours of opening. Supermarkets in the larger towns and cities tend to open all day now and the odd few one Sunday in every month, but then you have problem of which brand is most like the ones you are used to, being from a nation of tea drinkers for example tea in Italy has a tendency to taste more like cardboard, but I can vouch for the coffee.

Living as we do some thirty kilometres from the nearest large supermarket it is essential to plan your visit to combine the acquisition of all of your other needs in one day. Generally speaking that means between the hours of 8am and 1pm or 4pm and 8pm, depending on the type of shop you seek. If you fail to reach the shop before the 1pm deadline you either have to sit somewhere twiddling your thumbs for three hours until it opens again or return home until the next visit. Hardware stores are generally closed on Saturday afternoons and during siesta but the evening opening can extend until 8 or 9pm. Fuel stations are invariably closed during the siesta but to the uninitiated have complicated machines that allow you to dispense your own fuel, providing you can understand what the robotic voice within is saying.

So when Nick and I go off on a shopping trip we go armed with a comprehensive list, an opening timetable and an itinerary that would impress any logistics expert. On this occasion having visited Tatianna we needed diesel for Rover and an entirely different type of fuel for the chainsaw and garden strimmer. These two pieces of equipment are essential when living in rural Italy, the former to aid in the gathering of wood for the fires the latter to prevent the forest from claiming your garden as its own, which it does all too rapidly because of the ideal growing conditions. Both items run on what in England you would term as 2 stroke fuel, a mixture of fifty parts unleaded petrol to one part '2 stroke oil'.

Most rural garages or fuel stations will do the mixing for you. Indeed all of the service stations apart from the truly rural ones offer a two-tier system of service and the fuel is priced accordingly. In the self-service bay or *Fai Da Te* you fill your tank, check your oil and radiator liquids and if necessary clean your windscreen with the water and tools provided. The first time I entered I drove into the pump area marked *servito*, in ignorance of the system I admit, a cheerful young male attendant dressed like a formula one pit stop engineer, overalls festooned with *Agip* logos clinging to a robust and well shaped form, swooped on me. He tapped the window nodded at the ignition key saying '*quanto vuoi*', he then removed the filler cap placed the pump nozzle in the tank, switched to automatic at the predetermined level of fuel and returned to my window. He then tapped on the bonnet with the words *'aperto per favore',* open please, and then proceeded to carry out the other checks before finally cleaning the windscreen with a flourish. The last specks of insect deposits were searched for at close quarters and disposed of with a squeaking chamois drawn from the holster of tools strapped to his slim waist; all within the time it took for the tank to fill. At first I thought this activity was leading up to a cupped hand in search of a tip, but tipping is not generally an accepted practice here. A smile and a nod left me in no doubt that this particular attendant was merely taking a pride in his work. Refreshing, I thought until I came to pay the bill and realised I had been charged at the higher rate of roughly two *centesimi* more per litre, but then I guess it is tempting to use the service just for the entertainment alone....

*

Having arrived back at the Barn Nick and I looked through the mail which as you can imagine nearly always came from England as we had not yet completely severed all our ties. Some of the letters would arrive in fairly quick time others a few days outside of expected timescales one or two would arrive as much as ten days late and on occasions a Christmas card arrived in July and on another a 'Fathers Day' card posted in June from the Isle of Man, arrived in November. Letters we were expecting often didn't arrive at all; the only ones that never failed to arrive on time were the ones you didn't want to get, like tax demands. We have even sent letters to England where the contents had been removed; the envelope re-sealed and sent on its journey completely empty; a telephone call from my bemused father was the only evidence of a failed attempt to get a computer memory stick full of photographs to him.

Sometimes it is difficult to obtain certain items, for example washers for the taps. In England you simply made a trip to the DIY superstore, here however you first have to find a plumbing outlet, predominately the domain of tradesmen and as a woman you must then brave the stares and smirks as you ask for whatever it is you came for. We recently had a leaking tap in the bathroom and Nick being able to deal with most simple tasks embarked upon finding the offending washer in order to determine its size. With the well pump switched off he proceeded to remove the various screws and nuts only to find that the tap seemed to be completely sealed and access to the washer only possible using special tools. Having disconnected all the various components we had to travel thirty kilometres to the nearest trade outlet with the tap unit in several pieces to try and discover how to replace the washer. Here we would discover that we would have to replace the whole tap.

The assistant then proceeded to bring to the counter every available tap set he had in stock but was unable to supply an exact match. Consequently we had to travel another fifteen kilometres to Pieve Santo Stefano to the builder's merchant that supplied the original bathroom fittings, to try to obtain the one replacement tap that we needed. Much to our dismay the tap was now discontinued stock. Bearing in mind that most bathrooms in Italy have bidets and we didn't want to replace those taps as well, we settled for a pair of similar looking ones, at a staggering cost of one hundred and twenty five euros. When we arrived home Nick discovered that the fittings were completely different and it became necessary to employ the services of a plumber who charged another one hundred euros, cash with no receipt of course. In England the whole undertaking might have cost no more than ten pence.

Generally most items are available and if you can't find what you are looking for there is always Amazon, ordering is however one thing, delivery another. The private courier services are often worse than the state postal system. When delivering if unable to find a property they would simply return the item to the depot miles away, possibly as far away as Milan, where the item originally arrived by airfreight. Here it can sit for days before being reloaded for a second attempt.

The opening times of retail outlets, shops and offices is something that you come to learn over a period of time and I had made a list of as many as we had encountered along the way. It is a list that I recorded on my mobile phone and I keep it with me at all times and yet even then you can turn up and discover that they have changed the opening hours.

Even the local bank seems to have adopted a pleasantly relaxed attitude to its customers. On one occasion I went early to the bank, which is supposed to open at 8.20am, we had much to do that day and so thought we would be first in the queue and avoid a delay. On that particular morning however the staff had decided not to arrive on time and the branch eventually opened over an hour later.

The local people know that the only bank cashier in the branch leaves the office for his coffee break at 10.30am and he can be seen taking a casual stroll up the hill to *Il Boschetto* the local café bar come restaurant at that precise time. He will not be available to serve customers until after 11am. During this temporary interruption to the business of the day the branch manager sometimes takes over the till, but only if he is not interviewing in the office. I along with a number of other uninitiated customers once made the mistake of arriving during the 'coffee break' and whilst standing at the counter waiting, a queue developed behind me. There was no shuffling of feet, no frustrated sighs and no tut-tuts merely a few glances at the clock with the recognition of having judged the time wrong. Eventually the office door opened and the branch manager shook his client's hand in farewell and led him through the queue to the main door, which reminded me of a 'beam me up Scottie' transportation capsule similar to those seen on Star Trek. He then proceeded to the till to serve me with a smile. As he dealt with the transaction I tried to make polite conversation in my limited Italian. In England the weather was always the first topic that came to mind so I happened to mention that someone had told me it was going to snow, '*No, no, Signora*', he said and in the middle of processing my few items of business he switched his computer to the Internet for the local weather forecast. After turning the screen towards the counter the queue gathered around me, all staring at the screen shaking their heads in agreement; it wasn't going to snow...

We have encountered so many such wonderfully relaxed idiosyncrasies during our time here and every day we venture beyond the Barn there is something new to make us laugh. The Italian people are so wonderfully relaxed and with the balanced Mediterranean diet it is no wonder they live to a ripe old age. I am sure that I read somewhere that they are the third longest living nation behind that of the Japanese and the Icelanders.

*

In the half-light of dusk four deer, an adult male, female and two fawns visited the meadow beyond the Barn that evening. The television went off along with the room lights and we spent almost half an hour in silence just watching. The adults grazed the early spring grass their heads raised at intervals, their ears alert to the slightest sound whilst the youngsters chased and pounced on each other like young lambs. The adults tentatively approached the Barn heads turning from side to side as if trying to catch our whispers beyond the glass of the doors. Seeking out the better grass of the lawns around the Barn they came within the perimeter fence, no more than a few feet away from us. The male had become a regular visitor and I had nicknamed him Frankie, he seemed to have no fear, the others slowly gained confidence and one by one came closer. The grey of their winter coats hung from them in tatters and the new white fur of their underbellies and rear ends stood out in the failing light. Suddenly the grazing stopped and their heads were raised; with ears twitching and black moustaches sniffing the air they turned and moved beyond the fence. As if in no hurry they gathered at the edge of the meadow where they blended in with the mottled shadows of the forest behind them and within a blink of an eye they were gone. It was scenes like this that made some of the difficult times all worthwhile.

That night we settled down to a simple meal of sausages and white beans or *salsicce con fagioli bianco* with baked potatoes and leeks. *Fagioli* beans are part of the staple diet and are served in the local restaurants with sage and olive oil and sometimes cream, they are a hearty accompaniment and most welcome on a chilly evening. The sausages are good, the skins being filled with 100% meat and mixed with various herbs and garlic and occasionally wine. The meal was soon ready and we washed it down with a glass of Nick's favourite red wine, *Rosso di Montefalco* which is produced in Umbria in the small hill top town of Montefalco. The last traces of the cream sauce with a delicate hint of sage were mopped up with some traditional Italian bread from Puglia. Ok, it wasn't Tuscan but it was kinder on the teeth and I suppose more akin to that of an English bloomer loaf, crusty on the outside and soft on the inside. Bread plays a big part in the Italian diet; Michelangelo who was born less than four kilometres away from the Chestnut Barn in Caprese Michelangelo, once said 'I feast on wine and bread and what feasts they are'.

The restaurants or *ristorante* bake fresh bread using olive oil, rosemary, olives and sage and on occasion nuts, it is delicious and often served warm straight from the oven. I had also learnt an interesting food fact from an Italian friend about leeks; she told me that it was the Romans who had first introduced leeks to England. Trivia I know but it was amazing the little snippets of information you could pick up as you went along.

Towards bedtime we sat reminiscing about the year we had spent here, the projects we had undertaken and finished, some with ease and some mixed with anger and frustration, the outcomes not perhaps as we would have liked them to be. Looking back now we could manage a smile and a chuckle although at the time things had been different.

I had asked Nick to fix me up with a washing line and he had a spare length of scaffolding pole left over from the Wi-Fi installation project which he had sunk into the ground some twenty metres from the Barn. He now needed to fix the other end by drilling into the side of the *loggia* and inserting a dowel hook into the wall. He knew exactly what he needed to complete the job. The dowel had a hook on one end, a screw thread and an expanding raw-plug on the other which once positioned in the drilled hole, would expand as you turned the hook. It meant a trip to Sansepolcro and the *ferramenta*, hardware shop situated on the approach to the town.

As we turned into the car park space we happened to recognise a friend, Josh, he is a landscape gardener and lives here with his wife, Virginia and their two children beyond the town of Monterchi, in the nearby village of Fonaco. As we hadn't seen him for a while we were in the process of catching up with all the news as we walked. On approaching the main door I could see a large gathering of people close to the front of the counter and behind it a line of employees. There was a queuing system governed by the taking of a ticket and waiting until your number was either called out or appeared on a digital screen above the counter. An assistant would then dash about collecting together your purchases; you would settle the account and leave. I couldn't quite understand why there was no activity and the first thing that entered my mind was that somebody was holding up the store; had we arrived, robbery in progress?

Nick and Josh followed behind still in mid conversation and in a single file avoiding the various displays that littered the store floor. Oblivious to the silence they carried on walking and talking at normal volume. All of a sudden a huge globule of water passed over my head and struck Nick squarely in the centre of his forehead, the splat and cry of shock clearly audible in the silence. Immediately halting in the line, he shook his head and swiped a hand across his brow. All three of us were now silent and standing perfectly still. I glanced at the other occupants of the store and sheepish grins began to appear wherever I looked. Words spoken in Latin in that unmistakable monotone delivery of a priest broke the silence, and I could swear that he too was grinning behind his eyes as he continued officiating over the impromptu flock that stood before him. Holy water was now being splashed liberally around the room instead of being aimed deliberately in our direction.

We have since discovered that it is the custom for a priest to visit every one of his regular congregation on the run up to Easter and to bless their homes, but with many Italians out at work all day, home visits are impossible. The blessing is now given in a very different manner and we were witnessing it at first hand. We had come for a dowel hook and ended up more than we bargained for.

The next few days were uneventful, the weather was mild but damp with a penetrating drizzle that kept both of us happily in front of the wood burners; we had an excuse that we really didn't need, to do nothing. Clouds shrouded the meadow in the swirling mists that came and went so rapidly that one minute we looked upon the heights of Monte il Castello and the next upon a blank white canvas, lightly stained with the vague outlines of the oaks and chestnuts that we knew were there. Confined as we were, Nick continued to write about his grandfather's experiences as a Royal Marine in the Great War. The unforgettable horrors of Gallipoli were now committed to the page and tomorrow in the silence of the midnight hour his grandfather would be leaving the peninsular and on his way to France, and the Battle of the Somme.

# CHAPTER 5

It was nearing the end of March, the suns rays, which had seemed such a long time coming now brought a golden tinge to the remnants of autumn that still, clung to the forest. Long strands of spider's web drifted across the meadow on the light warm breeze that came down through the trees from the hills above us. Insects awakened by the warmth darted back and forth across lengthening grass that would soon come alive with the wild flowers we had sown when we first arrived. The banks and the paths we had cleared of brambles were now dressed with flourishing yellow clusters of primroses, carefully relocated from the forest glades just behind the Barn. Bulbs we had previously brought from England had survived the frosts, the snow and the porcupines. In a few weeks we would be looking out on daffodils and tulips; and hopefully the irises, a great favourite of porcupines and wild boar would follow soon.

The fruit trees we had planted, apples, plums and figs which incidentally had born one lonely fig and one rotten apple, were now bursting into life; the new leaves a vivid lime green to match those of the chestnut trees on the perimeter of the meadow. Before too long the oaks would cast off their deep brown canopies to offer a contrasting darker green and the dark winter boughs would disappear from view. Birds with the exception of an extremely friendly, Robin rarely stayed at this altitude during the colder months were singing for all they were worth. The gentle, mellow sound was spoilt only by a group of jays, squabbling and screeching; which echoed from deep within the forest.

In the cool of the early evening the melancholy sound of a Blackbird rang out, his song continued as dusk fell; he was desperate to find a mate. Suddenly my friendly deer Frankie who came to graze in the meadow disturbed him, his tune turned to a frantic alarm call sounded on the wing as he disappeared. He would return the following evening to begin this delightful ritual all over again. It took him at least two seasons to find a mate but it all paid off in the end.

Frankie was on his own, he made none of the usual deep throaty barking sounds as he approached, it was my turn to do all the talking and he stood, ears twitching grazing only metres away, undeterred by my constant chattering. He is a magnificent beast even though he is not fully mature; it would be sometime before he would be able to take on the competition, his antlers still slight protrusions just in front of each of his ears. By his third year he would have a full set of tines and a secondary branch but he would not be ready for the rut until his seventh year, if he survives that long. His blood curdling cries can often be heard at various times of the day always in close proximity to the Chestnut Barn, it is like a very loud ill-mannered burp. The call would attract other deer so they could settle together for the night, safety in numbers I suppose. They sleep near the Barn as we had seen the patches of grass and shrubbery flattened into small round hollows, their traces like rabbit droppings scattered in all directions. It is as if they feel safe here, somehow knowing we would not harm them. We had seen them leave in the light of the early hours and head off into the forest in search of fresh pasture, cutting a network of paths for their fellow deer to follow. We often mimicked Frankies' bark and he always replied; it was turning into quite a joke with our friends that we had a resident deer. I was turning into a female version of Doctor Doolittle, talking to and naming the animals or maybe it was the influence of St Francis of Assisi, Italy's patron Saint rubbing off on me, after all he had walked in the hills and mountains not far from the Chestnut Barn.

Within days the cuckoo was a welcome sight, often so close to the Barn that you can easily see the mottled stripes of its white and grey breast and the piercing orange of its eye. The sound of its call at first is a pleasant reminder that summer is near, but later becomes so relentless, that it often misses a note and sounds as if suffering with a bad bout of hiccups; eventually you feel like shooting it.

Our pair of resident black squirrels which I have fondly nicknamed Silvio and Sonata scamper up and down the chestnut trees chasing each other, jumping from branch to branch, the male not in the least bit shy about his intentions. It just seems to take forever, their tufted ears twitch and their tails shake incessantly during this courtship. When he catches up with her he seems to lose his nerve and the roles are suddenly reversed along with the darting about.

At this time of year the sun slips behind the Regina Ridge, a spur that runs to the west of Monte il

Castello, at around 4.30pm; both the ridge and the mountain are due south of the Barn. Immediately, coolness returns to the air and the setting sun bathes the hills to the east of us in a warm orange glow. The oaks and the chestnuts, still only partially clothed, cast long shadows over the landscape that rolls away in undulating curves towards the Tiber Valley, six hundred metres below and thirty kilometres away. We sit in the *loggia* and watch the changing colours as the day slips away; a gentle breeze disturbs the wind chimes, it's tune along with the sad song of the Blackbird are the only sounds that invade the silence.

After re-stocking the wood baskets and emptying the ashes from the draw of the wood burner Nick took a match to the small pile of dry kindling and lit a fire whilst I set about preparing dinner.

Most Italian chefs will tell you that the secret of Italian cooking at its best is based on using only fresh ingredients. The majority of vegetables are grown locally in the *orte,* but we are not yet sufficiently well established to have a plot to grow our own, and our nocturnal visitors would have a wonderful feast. We rely on the fresh foods that arrive locally every day, a large percentage of these come from Puglia in the south east of Italy, on the 'heel'. The wild boar or *cinghiale* have snouts that will put a plough to shame; repairing the evidence of their crimes becomes a regular pastime during the winter months. The adults can displace boulders that the two of us have failed to lift. The deep furrows in the lawn and the tufts of precious dislodged turf regularly require the skills of the landscape gardener

(Nick). I am almost suspicious when he says 'Just remember, they were here first.' I notice however that he tries to encourage the hunters during the shooting season, gesticulating in exasperation as he does towards the 'ploughed field' while shrugging his shoulders with the word *cinghiale* and pointing in the direction of the lane at the top of the meadow suggesting, 'they went that way'. He knows very well that I deplore hunting in any form.

The porcupine or *porcospino* we are told, are very partial to potatoes, but here at various locations around the Barn they dig incredibly deep holes usually where they are the least conspicuous and invariably on one of the paths for one of us to fall into. During the winter months they are probably after the roots of the trees we are trying to preserve; either that or they are planning on moving in on a permanent basis, living as they do in deep burrows. I hope they don't, I have to say as they can decimate a garden during one of their covert night attacks. The deer, well there is nothing they like more than to nibble the bark of the fruit trees and in the summer months tear the trailing geraniums from my carefully placed troughs, tossing them to one side in disgust before moving on.

Going back to food, I am told by one of my Italian friends that Italian larders consist of the following ingredients, oils and fat, balsamic and white wine vinegar, *pasta*, rice, *polenta*, and beans.

*Risotto* is a popular dish and only a few types of rice should be used, the one I tend to favour is *Arborio*. *Polenta* is another staple food; a cooked ground cornmeal that I first tasted whilst staying in the Italian Alps, it is a filling addition to meat, and I suppose you could liken it to that of a firm, savoury semolina. The older Italian ladies still use the traditional *farina di polenta* and make it from scratch which can take a long time to cook and needs stirring continuously. Today though in a world full of modern convenience foods, quick just add water versions can be bought and prepared in five minutes. Beans well they come either fresh from the pod, canned or dried; there are *cannellini*, *borlotti* and *bianchi*.

Dried breadcrumbs or *pane grattugiato* are a must have, and are added to stuffing's or used to coat meat or vegetables prior to frying. Chickpeas or *ceci* are another favourite and mainly used in soups, or to bulk out and thicken stews. *Pasta* you can buy in all different shapes and sizes either fresh or dried; there are far too many varieties to list.

Next there are tomatoes or *pomodori*, these are one of the most essential ingredients of Italian cookery and if not used fresh, can be preserved or bought in a number of ways. *Passata* is a bottled tomato sauce, there are canned tomatoes and of course *pomodori secchi* dried tomatoes, which have been cut in half, laid out under the sun and sprinkled with salt. These tend to be used to flavour sauces and soups or as part of an appetiser or *antipasto.* All varieties are widely available in local shops and supermarkets.

Culinary herbs grow wild in and around the Barn and we are lucky enough to have an abundance of wild mint and thyme. We also manage to grow basil and rosemary, which are both commonly used. Basil or *basilico*, is a wonderful green herb, vital for Italian cooking as it is used in the making of *Pesto*, a famous Italian sauce which when combined with any cooked *pasta* is delicious. Basil leaves can also be used in salads and are the key ingredient in the *Caprese* or *insalata tricolore*, the large fresh leaves give a piquant taste and compliment the sliced ripe juicy tomatoes and soft *mozzarella*. The colours of the ingredients represent the colours of the Italian flag. Here is a favourite recipe I use for the *Pesto* sauce.

*

## *Pesto sauce:*

55g fresh bruised basil leaves
3 crushed cloves of garlic
6 tbsp extra virgin olive oil
1 tbsp pine kernels
25g grated *Parmigiano*

Place all the ingredients into a blender and blitz until a smooth paste is formed or alternatively crush and mix using a pestle and mortar then once ready simply add to your cooked *pasta* ensuring that it is well covered.
Sprinkle with a little *Parmigiano* and serve immediately with warmed bread.

*

For now though, I was more concerned with preparing something quick and filling and *pasta* fell into that category perfectly. *Spaghetti Carbonara* is one of Nick's favourite dishes and consists of bacon and eggs with *pasta*. I had bought fresh *pancetta* from the local shop, it is a type of bacon infused with herbs, and I sliced it into cubes and fried it with diced onion and crushed garlic. Then I added the *pancetta,* onion and garlic to some cooked *spaghetti* and stirred in the beaten eggs and cream ensuring the eggs were fully combined, cooked, but did not resemble scramble egg. The whole dish was complete within minutes and once sprinkled generously with grated *Parmigiano* was ready to eat.

The next morning it was time to fly back to England. The past weeks had flown by, with much of our time spent settling back in to an Italian way of life. As we left for Perugia Airport, we drove down through the little village of Lama, past the mechanics and along the straight road that led to the DeSpar shop. We pulled in at a house that we knew was owned by an English couple, both of them were busying themselves on their driveway. We had often waved at them when passing but this time we stopped and introduced ourselves. Mick was a retired policeman and his wife Helen a retired head teacher. Helen had taken early retirement so they could both escape the North of England and live a more peaceful way of life, nestled amongst the Italian countryside. They too had bought their house a number of years ago and had lived there permanently for a number of years. Helen is fluent in Italian and on occasions teaches at the local secondary school or *liceo* in Sansepolcro. At the time, we were unable to stop for very long, our busy schedule calling, so we agreed that we would all meet up upon our return. Helen and Mick were soon to become very good friends.

Perugia airport was once a rather quaint, small, and quiet airport that had long been in the process of being updated to accommodate the extra traffic that now flows through it. Its situation is ideal for us, being less than an hour's drive from the Chestnut Barn. It also has the added advantage of free parking, a concession that would only be available during the reconstruction. Here the low cost airline 'Ryan air' runs three flights a week into London Stansted.

The sight of an abundance of English registered vehicles whose owners travelled from all over Italy to take advantage of this free parking had, until now always greeted us on our arrival. Usually they were parked in little groups together, as if their owners thought their cars might benefit from the comfort of having English company for the duration of their visit. This was a sight that always prompted 'Like ruddy Sainsbury's in here these days,' from Nick who firmly believed that cars attract cars, like magnets. He was usually right, he used to say that if you were to park in the far reaches of an empty car park, someone would always come and park next to you and then leave a little dent in your door as they left. To our surprise the construction was complete and all the usual paraphernalia associated with major works like cranes and concrete lorries had disappeared, along with the hoarding that had hidden the façade from view.

Before us was a very impressive building but on the lead up to it were a large number of less impressive signs guiding you towards the drop-off zone, the hire car zone, the taxi rank, the bus stop, but even more disconcerting was the sign that guided you towards the barriers of the long-stay car park and the ticket machines. There were now 'no parking' signs everywhere you looked, the English cars were conspicuous by their absence and the Italians had parked just about anywhere that the airport authorities had failed to place a sign or a prohibitive line along a curb. One or two vehicles even appeared to have been casually discarded on the central green of the roundabout in front of the airport gates. The grass verges had disappeared under the volume of Italian cars both inside and out, the whole area looked like a massive scrap-yard. Needless to say the allocated beautifully prepared parking bays stood empty; apart that is from the newly arrived Rover.

Nine days in all were spent in England, Nick sorting out his work issues, whilst I spent time that seemed to pass all too quickly, with my mum and dad. We returned to Italy on the 17$^{th}$ April and immediately began to prepare for the much-awaited visit of Nick's son Stephen, his wife Angela and our two wonderful grandchildren, Chloe and Max. We had just four days. The Barn needed a spring clean and the lounge walls a coat of paint; sooty deposits from the wood-burner had left dark shadows in the corners and around the beam ends, it clung to cobwebs nestling between the cross beams that I had failed to notice until the spring sunshine filled the room. I had mistakenly tried to wash the walls; the result was a total disaster. We would have to consider how to get around this problem in future years, as having to decorate at the end of every autumn-winter season would be an unwelcome task.

Nick and I being adept at most things completed the work in a day and Nick even managed to find the time to climb up onto the roof and sweep the chimney. He then made a fireguard with chicken wire stretched over a wooden folding frame, which opened out to make a U shaped surround. Although rustic in appearance it was enough to ensure Chloe and Max would be a safe distance from the wood burner when it was lit during the evenings. Trying to find one to buy not only proved impossible, but also so time consuming that we eventually gave up.

*

The Barn, situated as it is in the Apennine Mountain range and in an area that is subject to the occasional earthquake, received special attention during its reconstruction. The original stonewalls to the main barn were lined with seismic blocks and the swimming pool was built on a steel frame that was positioned on a special raft that would ride over any tremors we might experience. I mention this now because most people are aware that Italy suffers more than most European countries with earthquakes

69

and with the devastation they can leave behind. Twenty-six people died during May 2012 and widespread damage was caused to many architecturally important buildings in and around the Emilia Romagna region. The first quake registered a magnitude of 5.9, two after shocks then followed at a magnitude of 5.2. Another quake registering 5.8 followed just nine days later causing even more deaths and considerable damage. The effects were felt as far away as the region of Aosta in northern Italy and parts of Austria, Switzerland and Croatia.

Tremors are common, we have felt the odd one ourselves although not at the Chestnut Barn; it has to be said that rarely are the effects evidenced by structural damage, and it may well have happened once or twice while we were asleep. The sensation is no more startling than what you might expect if a large lorry rumbles past your property causing vibration, although quakes and tremors can last much longer.

We made the decision to live in this region of Tuscany knowing the facts and would never have been put off, the property was rebuilt to withstand such occurrences and until recently the State picked up the tab for repairing properties so damaged. Now though you must make sure that your own property insurance contains a clause specifically relating to earthquake damage. The real-estate agent who sells you an Italian property will convey none of these facts to you.

All of this is mentioned because the day before the family arrived we received an email from our

English friends David and Ernest who have a home situated just within the ancient walls of Citta Di Castello. They live in London for most of the year but also spend quite a bit of time here in their beautiful three-storey townhouse. The property has a wonderful courtyard garden under the city wall, so beautifully kept that it might have come straight out of the pages of 'Homes and Gardens'. The property also has a private roof-terrace tiled in terracotta, a haven amongst the chimney pots. It is accessed via the third floor bedroom and looks out over the medieval city and the rolling Umbrian hills beyond. The house is full of valuable treasures of antique furniture and Objet d'art that both David and Ernest have collected over the years.

Their e-mail mentioned in passing that there had been an earthquake at ten o'clock that morning; according to the seismic observatory it had measured 3.6 on the Richter scale at the epicentre. The tremor had shaken the house leaving all of David's beautiful pictures and artwork hanging at obscure angles around the rooms; nothing had been broken and no structural damage was in evidence. We all accept that it happens here and nobody is too alarmed by it. Citta Di Castello still stands like it has for that last eight hundred years and will probably stand for another eight hundred years. It is only forty-two kilometres from the Barn along the E45 highway; we had felt nothing, and this was a fair size tremor.

*

Later that morning we left the Chestnut Barn for Sansepolcro and the *supermercato* where we would stock up on food and buy more wine to replenish our dwindling reserves, ready for our family's imminent arrival. The drizzle from the previous day had miraculously vanished, blue skies, sunshine and that fresh earthy smell that follows the rain is a welcome treat for the senses to savour. There was no need to hurry; there are no deadlines, no meetings to attend, no piles of paperwork staring us in the face; just a quick tour of the garden to check on the progress of the flowers, look at the primroses, and replace the few clods of turf that may have been disturbed during the night, this was our rush hour now.

When you travel through the villages on mornings like these you have the opportunity to check out everybody's bed linen, coloured duvets, sheets and even pillows are draped over windowsills everywhere you look. It reminded me of those special flag days like the Queen's diamond jubilee. I was half expecting to see long trestle tables festooned with plastic union jacks, white linen tablecloths, paper plates and plastic cutlery, just around the next bend.

It is a familiar sight here in Italy, the bedding airing in the warm sunshine; it bought a smile to my face as I conjured up images of those passionate Mediterranean nights that might have preceded this customary practice. The romantic images that ran through my mind were soon dashed by the sight of an elderly lady barely able to walk, let alone indulge in such...we'll say no more. The rustic witch style broomstick was the only thing holding her up.

While my thoughts were, as you might say in the realms of fantasy there was a tremendously loud bang that came from beneath Rover; it sounded and felt like the bottom had fallen out. Nick stopped immediately, in truth he had no alternative as the rear wheels had completely seized and there was a trail of black rubber running for ten yards behind us. We looked at each other in disbelief and panic; we jumped out quickly to see if there was anything obvious lying in the road, like the engine.

The elderly lady was no longer busily sweeping her entrance; she stood with one hand clasped to her breast and her mouth open in shock. She was so stooped, poor lady that she merely had to tilt her head to one side to see if there was anything under the car; I was beginning to wonder if she would survive the experience.

She wore an old fashioned blue stripped housecoat over her skirt and jumper, her legs were covered with thick woolly tights and her hair was neatly pulled back, tied and covered with a floral headscarf. Judging by the curvature of her back and the deep lines etched into her kindly face, she must have been well into her nineties if not a hundred. She was now staring at us with a deep frown and a look of concern in her eyes, words hurried from her mouth and at first I thought she was remonstrating with us for nearly causing her to have a heart attack.

None of what she was saying was making any sense and I can only guess that she may have been speaking in a local dialect, which is not uncommon in these parts. I smiled and nodded; pretending to understand as she continued chattering and making forward motions, I just hoped she wasn't going to ask me a question that warranted an answer. Her hands were gesticulating and pointing down the hill, the only word I managed to decipher was 'Ennio,' the name of the local mechanic.

Nick had laid an old blanket on the ground and was partially under Rover with one leg waving about in a similar fashion to the old lady's arms as he tried to manoeuvre his body through the tight gap between Rover and the road. A few minutes later, while I was nodding, smiling and acknowledging the old lady with the occasional *Sì sì*, he re-emerged, his face now covered in oil and grease with a silent expletive on his lips. He can do most things but he can't do cars.

"There's a \******* hole in the differential" he said.

Of course I had no idea what this meant, I was more concerned that the internationally understood Anglo Saxon word that had slipped so casually from his lips had not been understood by this dear old lady. By the look on her face, the nod, the smile and the, 'ah, *Sì'* that followed I could see she was fortunately none the wiser.

Once safely fastened back in Rover we said our goodbyes and Nick cautiously started the engine, released the handbrake and with the engine in neutral, just in case it was the gear box that had made us grind to a halt he allowed gravity to take over, and we slowly at first, started to roll down the steep mountain road. The problem was that the garage was off the main road to the right and the final seventy-five metres ran up a steep incline. So we had to build up enough speed to make the hill. I will not go into too much detail, except to say that I was petrified, Rover sounded like an old tractor and the clonking that was coming from the rear forced me to put my fingers in my ears. People stood by the side of the road to watch us pass and a builder, re-pointing the stonework on a nearby house nearly fell off the scaffolding. Suddenly the noise ceased as if something metal had released itself and the last stages were negotiated with breathtaking speed. We hit the incline with another loud bang and I swear that Rover left the ground for a few seconds before coming to rest half way up the drive. By this time the occupants of the garage had been fully alerted.

Ennio appeared from under the bonnet of an ageing but still capable blue Fiat Panda. Nick having walked the rest of the way tried to explain with a wet finger and a diagram in the dust on the Fiat's bonnet that he thought there was a hole in the differential, Ennio told us to leave Rover where he was: he would tow him the rest of the way and would have a look at him later that day. Ennio's wife Miranda suddenly appeared from beneath a different bonnet her face, like Nick's smeared with oil and grease. She immediately recognised us as the mad couple that lived in the forest and without hesitation offered us a lift back up to the Chestnut Barn. She knew exactly where it was, all the locals did, they all knew of the house in the woods with the swimming pool…Miranda explained that she was familiar with the track that led up to the Barn being a regular fungi picker during the spring and autumn months.

Nick and I clambered up into the front seat of an extremely old khaki coloured 4x4, that looked like something that might have survived from the second world war, what make or model it was, I have no idea. It started at the first turn of the key and it saved us from walking the three and half kilometres back up the mountain and home. As we passed the cemetery on the sharp bend at Colle di Fragaiolo, Miranda, as if on auto pilot made the sign of the cross against her body, with one hand holding the steering wheel, I said to Nick that I'll have to remember to do that the next time we shoot past at seventy miles an hour with no engine and gear box to help slow us down.

*

Stephen and Angela were flying into Bologna Airport and would now have to find their own way to the Chestnut Barn. Chloe and Max were older and both walking, which meant hopefully it would be less of a struggle trying to juggle their luggage and the pushchair around the airport. Steve had had the foresight to reserve a seven-seater car for the two weeks of their stay as we had some trips and sightseeing planned and it made sense travelling together. Maybe this would be the solution to our transport problem until Rover was repaired.

Ennio and Miranda's daughter, Ilaria spoke and wrote a little English and as my Italian was still not up to translating the names of the parts of a car engine and other technical terms I thought it would be easier if we corresponded by way of e-mails. When she didn't have the correct English translation I would use a certain software application and translate the Italian equivalent into English. The offending part was indeed the rear differential; the clonking sound was the rear axle turning the steel components of the differential into iron filings. The cost of a replacement was going to be somewhere in the region of 1,300 euros and that was without labour.

Our Freelander 1 (Rover) had long since become a bit of a standing joke with our friends and family as over the years we had worked out that on a car we had purchased new, we had spent more than half of his original cost on repairs. We have had to replace the catalytic converter, the clutch, the fuel injectors twice and a number of hoses had failed just at the most inconvenient time, I could go on and on but I won't bore you with the details. Somebody once told us that we had purchased not only the worst Land Rover model ever made, but also the worst car ever made; I can well believe it. Nick and I had discussed trading him in on many occasions but felt that there was really no point, the bodywork was still in good order and in any case who would be daft enough to take him?

Where as at one time we would have used genuine Land Rover parts we now buy OEM (Original

Equipment Manufacturer) parts and have them shipped across from England, these are a fraction of the cost even with the shipping fees. Labour costs here in Italy are considerably cheaper by the hour; even the main dealerships are more than a third of the price of their British counterparts and the smaller mechanics like Ennio are half that again. He charges twenty-two euros an hour; in England you could pay as much as £140.00 per hour. After ordering the parts an estimated delivery date was established and I responded to Ilaria advising her of our actions.

Sunday morning arrived and we sat excitedly at home waiting for a text from Angela to say that they had landed safely. They were flying with British Airways from London Gatwick so we hoped there would be no delays. Nick and I were always a little anxious when they flew into Bologna, as we had never forgotten the strange incident that had taken place one previous summer...

Bologna is a busy airport and we had felt it would be easier for Stephen and Angela who had travelled all the way from the Isle of Man with two small children, to have us both on hand at the arrival lounge to look after the children while they retrieved their luggage and sorted out the rental car. An hour later we were all travelling along the A14 highway heading east towards Cesena.

This normally busy road was fairly quiet it being a Sunday and the time of day when the majority of Italians are having a family lunch. We were enjoying a delightful rendition of Baa, Baa Black Sheep from Chloe who was strapped in her car seat in the back when the journey took an unexpected turn of events. Nick had passed a fairly old, pale blue Renault with two young Italian men occupying the driver and front passenger seats. For some reason as soon as we had passed the vehicle the driver accelerated and proceeded to pull up in front of us with a view to slowing us down. Incidentally we were keeping well within the speed limit. Nick had to brake hard and in no mood for motorway high jinks especially with a three year old in the back, gave one or two unconventional hand signals; you probably know the ones I mean. Fortunately Chloe was asleep by now.

Nick passed the car again and thinking they might have missed his meaning repeated the signals, only this time more vigorously. The expressions on their faces left me in no doubt that the message had been received. Having once again completed the overtaking manoeuvre the blue Renault pulled alongside, the passenger wound down his window and indicated to me that I should do the same; bearing in mind we are right hand drive he began speaking to me in Italian but even before he had opened his mouth that old international Anglo Saxon word was wending its way across the void, spoken with considerable venom and indeed volume. At this point the first of two Police identity cards were pressed to the window with clear instruction for us to pull over. Nick was by now furious and ready for a confrontation.

'Police don't drive clapped out Renaults' he said, and as we pulled over we locked all of Rover's doors. Nick refused to open his window by more than an inch. I went into panic mode; Nick went into fighting mode, although I don't know what he thought he was going to do against two fit young men. 'Leave it,' I said, 'you never know he could have a knife, he could stab you.' Meanwhile, Stephen, Angela and Max who had been following close behind and had witnessed all of this, pulled off the road leaving a short distance between us. Stephen obviously slightly confused but ready to assist his dad at the first sign of trouble began to run towards us. The driver of the Renault left his vehicle and walked over to Nick's window where he casually waved another police identity card, I remember seeing some sort of hologram but it was flashed so quickly I only caught a fleeting glimpse and I could not be sure of its authenticity. Leaning towards the tiny gap in our window he asked in Italian if we were English and thinking that it might possibly help the situation, I responded without hesitation in Italian. I told him that my husband was English and that I was Italian.

Unsurprisingly and within seconds of my response he was back seated in his car with his passenger and they sped off. If they were police, they were certainly undercover police, but of course I have my doubts. I have heard stories of such happenings before that have resulted in the theft of valuables, suitcases and the all important documents that you must have in your possession when travelling in Italy, such as passports or identity cards for each passenger along with vehicle ownership papers and insurance certificate. They were wearing the customary pair of standard issue 'Ray Ban' aviator sunglasses but with none of the stereo typical designer uniform associated with that of the *Carabineri* or *Polizia*. Maybe the fact that I had said that I was Italian had dissuaded them but in the heat of the moment neither of us had the foresight to record the vehicle registration plate with a view to reporting the incident. Nick just said 'Must be Starsky and Hutch, the car was old enough' and dear Chloe slept through the whole episode.

*

My mobile phone beeped and flashed simultaneously as a message popped up from Angela saying that they had just reached the Cesena Nord interchange and were passing through the large tollgates heading south towards Roma on the E45. The road is infamous for all the wrong reasons with unexpected potholes, lumps and bumps and shifting tarmac. It is a narrow dual carriageway that winds its way south from Cesena through the Apennine mountain range finally coming to an end at Orte. It seems that no matter what time of year it is, there is always some sort of repair being carried out. There are detours off the carriageway onto the old mountain road to avoid sections demanding major structural repairs. The mountain roads wind their way through hidden villages and deep pine tree lined ravines that are beautiful, but if you find yourself stuck behind a large lorry, these little diversions can take hours.

The mountains are continuously shifting, causing cracks and fissures on the tarmac surface, and this combined; with the searing heat of the Italian summers, followed by the weight of snow and freezing temperatures in winter, make it all the more difficult to maintain. Much of the route stands on a high, continuous viaduct that spans the valleys and riverbeds, an engineering feat to be admired, if it wasn't nearly always covered in scaffolding. The views on this stretch are breathtaking, if you dare to take your eyes off the road for a second, inadvisable as there is little to separate you from the landscape other than thin steel crash barriers that give the impression that they wouldn't hold a go-cart back. The steel expansion tracts on the viaduct run at fifty metre intervals and the booming sound as you pass over them is akin to a regular heartbeat, almost hypnotic in fact; not a road to drive on late at night especially if you are tired. An hour on the E45 is sufficient for anyone.

By half past four our guests had arrived at the Barn, and they were unpacked and seated in the sunshine under the pergola. The sound of a drilling woodpecker in the pine trees below, echoed through the stillness of the afternoon it drummed as if on a hollow bough, until it was finally disturbed by the children's laughter and it moved off to another part of the forest, the sound now distant, solitary.

Glasses of wine were emptied, bowls of nibbles refilled whilst the children played. They laughed and laughed as Max poured water from the garden hose into a watering can then proceeded to throw it over his granddad, who in mock protestation ran about the garden like a fourteen year old while they chased him with anything they could find that would hold water. I knew as the rest of us chatted that they would have Nick's undivided attention for the whole of the time they were here. He adored all of his grandchildren and from the moment they woke until the last of the bedtime stories he would be kicking or catching a ball, playing hide and seek or making regular trips up to the gazebo at the top the meadow; now a fine castle with a prince and princess and together they would fight dragons in the forest until the sun went down. I also knew that this was what he would miss the most by being so far away from them, these cherished but transient moments. This, I believed would be the biggest threat to his happiness, the distance from his boys and their families. I had been the driving force behind the move here, I was the one who motivated him towards a no going back decision but had I been so focused on my own aspirations that I had overlooked this potential stumbling block? Only time would tell...

# CHAPTER 6

When Nick had his unfortunate accident two years ago, he had lain in bed for over two weeks unable to move for fear of his life. His bed was situated next to the window in Sansepolcro hospital; from here he spent hours staring out at the beautiful Umbrian horizon and wishing himself there. The most prominent feature of those distant hills is the fortified town of Monte Santa Maria in Tiberina and he swore that once he was able to walk again he would visit the town that had been the focus of his determination for so long.

Now we were going to realise his ambition, taking the family for a day out which would include a long Italian style lunch in a restaurant that had been recommended to us by friends. The town is situated some forty kilometres northwest of Perugia, just over the Tuscan/Umbrian border, a little over fifty kilometres from the Barn.

It is no exaggeration to say that this is one of the most delightfully picturesque towns that we have visited; to describe the view from the top as spectacular is an understatement. It is referred to in an ancient 17th century poem as 'A Mountain that nearly borders with Heaven'. The small town can be seen for miles around, standing as it does on an isolated pinnacle, high above the ridge of the same name. To the north and south there is an almost vertical drop down to the river valley below. The approach from the east and west is along an exposed and unusually narrow ridge that cuts through some wonderful countryside. The chestnut and oak forests that line the routes are interspersed with patches of olive groves and vineyards. This was once the ancient territory of the Marquis of Bourbon, one of the oldest families in central Italy, his tomb can be found in the family chapel in the church of Santa Maria.

The palace or *Palazzo Boncompagni Ludovisi* the one time residence of the Marquis, sits shadowing the *piazza* and the castle of the same name. The *palazzo,* was built in the 1500's on the site of a former castle, it later fell into disrepair and was heavily damaged during the Second World War. It was not until the 1990's that the municipality acquired the building for restoration. Three of the ground floor rooms now house an exhibition entitled 'A Feud in the Imperial' which details the history of the territory, from its origins to the Marquis of Bourbon of Monte Santa Maria. There are also artefacts relating to the local area that date from the period between the Neolithic and 18th century. The exhibition is open to the general public everyday from July to September and by prior appointment from October to June. In 1250, an important year in Monte Santa Maria's history, the Marquis Guido, descendent of the previous owner, attacked the castle with a group soldiers, conquered it and established a new state.

The Marquisate of Monte Santa Maria was destined to last a good five and a half centuries. In fact, only the Papal State, the Republic of Venice, and the Dukedom, which later became the Kingdom of Savoy, managed to remain independent for longer. Thanks to their political skill, the owners of Monte Santa Maria obtained concessions and privileges from popes and emperors, enabling them to hold important public office in the nearby towns. Monte Santa Maria in Tiberina was free to have its own laws, to create alliances and to declare war, to receive legations, to mint its own coins, to impose taxes and to administrate justice by itself – its council therefore had absolute independence and self-rule. Monte Santa Maria was also one of the last three places in Europe along with Verona and Petersburg where it was possible to carry out duels to the death. It was later in the fifteenth century that the Marquises of Monte Santa Maria acquired the name 'Bourbon' from the King of France.

On leaving the *piazza* we found the ancient church of Santa Maria that was built in the first half of the 11th century it houses an unusual octagonal stone font dating back to the year 1000, as well as the private chapel of the Marquis di Bourbon family.

As we continued, the ancient cream coloured stone walls that towered above us oozed a feeling of warmth as well as radiating an almost yellow hue. Huge old wooden doors with pierced iron studs stand proud within stone porticoes; it was like travelling back to medieval times, something which the townsfolk of Santa Maria in Tiberina still do today when re-enacting events in their annual festivals that are held during the summer months.

Chloe and Max stood mesmerized by the intricately forged iron doorknockers, some depicting the heads of fierce lions, others of wild boar. The solid stonewalls still home to the wrought iron rings once used for tethering horses and livestock. We passed beneath the medieval arch, which at one time would have been the main entrance to the castle, on down the narrow stepped street, where to our delight we found the small family run restaurant, a welcoming outside terrace and yet more unforgettable views as far as the eye could see.

*

On a clear day your vision will take you as far south as the snow capped peaks of the *Gran Sasso d'Abruzzo*, (280 kilometres away) when translated means great stone of Abruzzo; it is the highest peak within the Apennine mountain range standing at over 2,900 metres. It is here on a plateau between the three main summits, known as

*Campo Imperatore* that you can find the hotel where it is said that Benito Mussolini was imprisoned during the August and September of 1943, before being freed by Nazi commandos. The *Monti Della Laga National Park*, in which these mountains lie, covers an area of 150,000 hectares and was established in 1991. It is home to semi wild horses and a number of wild animals including the Marsican brown bear, the Apennine wolf, Golden Eagles, Goshawks, Peregrine falcons to name but a few as well as other rare species of flora and fauna. The park also boasts a modest ski resort mainly frequented by Italian weekend skiers from Rome.

*

With our table chosen and the large cream canvas parasol raised to the sky, we browsed the menu. One thing I have noticed about the restaurants in Italy, there is never any mention of a 'children's menu', I have now learnt that this is because Italian children eat exactly the same as their parents, just a smaller portion. Cooking two different meals, one for the adults and one for the children is just not an option. Table etiquette is taught from an early age and I guess that is why we see so many children out late at night dining with their parents, they sit patiently at the table until late into the evening, to them it is a normal event. Fortunately for us Chloe and Max love *pasta* so after picking a suitable flavour sauce to compliment it, our orders were placed. Chloe by now was back playing her 'please and thank you game', without any prompting from me she tried it out on the waitress who beamed with delight upon hearing Chloe say 'thank you' in Italian. The Italians love children and no sooner had she disappeared inside with our order than she returned with two lollipops....

With the time fast approaching one o'clock the air filled with the mouth-watering aroma of freshly cooked *Porchetta* and as if by magic, the restaurant terrace began to fill with lunchtime diners. A larger table nearby had been reserved it was laid to accommodate eight and within minutes it was filled with working men who came for the *Operaio*, a set menu, normally comprising a *pasta* dish, meat with chips or salad together with water and a glass of wine. The cost is usually in the region of twelve euros per person; most of the rural restaurants and bars offer a similar lunch which helps to keep the tables full during the off peak season. Similar tourist menus advertising a sample of the local fare are also widely available.

The men arrived in high spirits and the otherwise tranquil atmosphere was rapidly transformed into good-natured banter, initially aimed at the laughing waitress. Eventually and inevitably their banter turned to football *calcio* the supporters of the winning side teasing those of the losing team. Intermingled around the table, winners and losers argued and gesticulated, where goals had been missed, the margin was expressed with arms widely spread, the laughter getting louder as losing heads slumped, shaken in resignation much to the elated cheers of their mocking rivals. The sports section of the local *Corriere dell'Umbria* newspaper showing the winning goal, was flung around the table like a game of pass the parcel, when the food arrived a quiet calmness returned to the terrace.

We could do nothing but laugh along with these friendly full of fun strangers, our amusement catching their attention forced a round of *Buongiorno* from everyone and we were soon firm friends. A few spots of rain later, a bit of furniture shuffling from the 'workmen's table' and we were, side by side, two tables squeezed under one parasol. The canopy just about sheltered us all from the huge droplets that briefly splattered onto the terrace. Rays of sunlight burst from behind the isolated and offending black cloud and the strange light brought the forests, olive groves, castles and terracotta roof tiles alive with colour, we weren't going to miss a second of the changing scene spread out before us. Bodies were now leaning right and left as droplets found their way down the backs of shirt collars; nobody wanted to move we were all having too much fun, and the moment, like the cloud, passed all too quickly. Our meals were brought to the table, the local Umbrian red wine poured. The words *Salute* and *Buon appetito*, meaning good health and enjoy your meal said to us by our unexpected dinner companions was reciprocated in broken Italian, the laughter it induced was with us and not at us.

On leaving the *piazza* and Monte Santa Maria in Tiberina behind, we negotiated the hairpin bends on a downward spiral and spotted two memorials to those that fell during both the Great War and the Second World War. We stopped and wound down the car windows taking time to reflect, whilst reading the names aloud. At least three members of one family were tragically killed during WW2, one as young as five years old. It was on days like these that times gone by were brought to the fore and I became eager to learn more of the history of the places we had visited.

*

Perugia Airport now the destination of 'Ryan air' flights from London Stansted was a captured wartime airfield from which allied aircraft flew regular sorties, in support of the advancing British Eighth Army. Field Marshall Albert Kesselring was overall commander of the Nazi armies in Italy, during the allied advance from the south he had ordered his forces to retreat in stages to a number of strategically situated strongholds that stretched across the land from coast to coast. These heavily defended lines built mainly by Italian slave labour, in some cases amounted to specially constructed defences situated on the highest peaks in the landscape, from where machine gun posts and artillery bunkers commanded the best view of the allied approach. Other links in the chain relied upon the beautiful hill towns, ready made for slowing down an attacking force. Monte Santa Maria in Tiberina was one such town in the chain of defences that later became known as the Arno Line. Kesselring's instructions were to fall back, fight, fall back and once again make a stand. A stand was made at the town.

A Ghurkha reconnaissance squad was approaching the area on the 11th July 1943 when it stumbled upon a Nazi bathing party. An Italian woman gave the alarm as the Ghurkhas raced in with their knives, the nudists apparently fled in all directions; six unfortunate soldiers were caught and shown no mercy when trying to make their escape. A Nazi Major wrote in his diary of his nervousness at the approach of his enemy's forces and of the intense sadness he felt at the loss of his men in such tragic circumstances. By now he had taken his troops to within the walls of Monte Santa Maria in Tiberina to await the arrival of the Ghurkhas and the tanks of the Warwickshire Yeomanry.

A fierce battle took place throughout the day on the 11th of July the defending forces dug in and successfully beat off the first of the British 10th Indian Division attacks, but by nightfall on the 12th July 1943, the town was surrounded. Under cover of darkness however the Nazi major and his men had managed to escape and retreat through British lines to the hamlet of Cagnano. After carrying out Kesselring's fight and fall back tactics they moved further north where after fighting on the plains of Monterchi, they would eventually find themselves on the heights of Monte il Castello above the Chestnut Barn fighting alongside the Jager Division and the remnants of the Panzer Grenadier

Division. The Chestnut Barn is due north of the mountain, it would have been in the direct line of the retreating Nazi Divisions that were forced to vacate the mountain by way of the Regina ridge; Nick often finds fragments of World War II shells and spent bullets whilst digging in the garden.

*

On the way home we stopped athe post office or *la Posta*, to send off some postcards. In Italy you can buy stamps for postcards at the tobacconists or *Tabaccheria* or at shops displaying the *Bollo* sign, alternatively you can go direct to the *Posta*. The local smaller offices tend to be open in the mornings only, whereas the main depots are open all day.

Once back at the Chestnut Barn we enjoyed the last hours of warm sunshine before the long tree-shadows once again striped the landscape in gold and lime green. As the sun finally disappeared behind the mountain the air freshened so we took refuge in front of the wood burners. The days are longer and warmer now, but the evenings seem to cling to the easterly wind and the temperature plummets as darkness falls. The supplies of cut logs will last until the heat of early summer drives away the evening chill, but for now an hour or two of vigorous flame and dying embers will warm the Barn long into the night.

The following day was an Italian holiday, the 25<sup>th</sup> April, the date when Italians celebrate the liberation of Italy after WWII. On days like this, almost every shop and supermarket will be closed, knowledge of these special days is essential so as to prepare well in advance. It is not just about keeping the larder full but if you are intending to eat out either at midday or in the evening you may find it impossible to find a table if you haven't booked well in advance. If you are planning a trip out in the car be aware that the roads also fill with energetic cyclists dressed in tight fitting Lycra, invariably in the Italian national sporting colours of blue and white. Bottoms pointing to the sky, odd shaped crash helmets fixed on the horizon, they sway from side to side as they take on the challenge of the steep mountain roads. They make a fine spectacle rather like salamanders fleeing from prey, but at five abreast they can also create a frustrating obstacle. They usually travel at speeds not quite fast enough for a car going up hill but on the downward slopes they can keep pace, making overtaking them quite a challenge.

The weather continued to be kind to us and we ventured out on foot to walk from La Faggeta around the north facing slopes of Monte il Castello to reach Sasso di Regina, the ridge opposite the Chestnut Barn. Until you reach the top of the mountain there is no way of knowing that on the summit there are wide open fields surrounded by tall beech trees that fall away towards Arezzo on one side and Caprese Michelangelo on the other. A saddle like depression where a fierce battle was fought during WWII spreads out before you and links the two main mountains, Monte Altuccia and Monte il Castello. It is difficult to imagine in these beautiful surroundings just how terrible it must have been when intensive fighting, bombing and shelling had turned this ground into total devastation. The area is frequented by people roaming with metal detectors looking for the bullets, shell fragments, badges of rank and the wreckage of the unimaginable that frequently rise to the surface as the mountain gently moves. Now the odd tree dotted here and there, patches of *ginestra* try to cover the deep scars of war. Nature has miraculously transformed craters into picturesque pools of water sitting in peaceful woodland glades, which look to have been there forever. Picnicking families sit in the glades and Italian lovers secrete themselves amongst the trees.

The approach to the top of the ridge is mainly uphill the track runs through the forest on the side of a sun-drenched saddle. Fresh new leaves overhang the path forming a tunnel of dappled light that twists and turns away into the distance. To the right far below on the mountainside there are signs of trenches and gun emplacements and if you search the forest floor hard enough there are odd pieces of shrapnel littered about. Once at the top we came across two Italian men they had a metal detector and were searching the outer perimeter of the woods, in broken Italian I managed to ask if they had found anything of interest. The men showed us their mornings finds, there were bullets, pieces of shrapnel and an old green glass wine bottle which was still as pristine as they day it had been made, on the bottom blown within the glass were the words 'Made in England'.

We made our way westwards to Monte Altuccia and steadily uphill to the small monument, which commemorates those that had fought for Italy's freedom.

Partisans had lived in these woods and prepared the way for the Allied soldiers who passed through here on their way north taking the city of Arezzo in their wake. The people of Valboncione harboured some of these men within their own homes, a dangerous practice as many fascist sympathisers lived in the area. We have heard stories of captured partisans being forced to dig their own graves by the side of the road before being shot.

We had been walking for well over an hour and bearing in mind we had the grandchildren with us we decided to turn and begin the trek back down to the car. On route Angela bent to pick up something metal from the path, it was the broken fragments of a hand grenade, two or three perfect cubes of steel that could rip a man to pieces. One the men out metal detecting may well have dropped it, but the area is covered in such artefacts even after so many years have passed.

For lunch we drove into Anghiari, to Bar Baldaccio, its name taken from the main square or *piazza* a favourite of ours because of its informality and an ideal place to take the children. We have known proprietors Maurizio and his wife Carla for a number of years, and they along with Fernando always greet us like long lost friends; a welcoming smile, a kiss on each cheek and a firm handshake for the men. Their disposable paper place settings depict ancient scenes of the town and the famous lost fresco by Leonardo Da Vinci of the *Battaglia di Anghiari*, which took place in 1440. The grandchildren love it here because they are presented with colouring pens to take on the task of adding colour to the scenes on the place settings. The *Pizza's* here are great, so too are the hamburgers, chips and hotdogs which always go down well with the children. Carla is a fantastic chef and also makes the most beautiful birthday cakes that are remarkable, both visually and gastronomically. Carla can produce a cake themed on pretty much anything you desire and can even replicate the composition of a photograph.

The restaurant overlooks the square from a slightly elevated position on the hill and from here you look towards the huge and prominent statue of Garibaldi with his arm raised supposedly pointing in the direction of Roma. The inscription on the plinth below reads *Roma o Morte*, Rome or die the finger however seems to point to the north, entirely the wrong direction for the capital city.

*

As the sun sets on this is a beautiful little medieval fortified town that rises up from the plain below, the spotlights hidden from view during the day come alive all along the defensive walls and beyond to the towers; the sight is quite something. When we had first negotiated the purchase of the Chestnut Barn with all the technicalities involved, it had been the place where we had stayed. During the evenings we often took a stroll through the enchanting streets, where the heat from the day continues to radiate from the stone late into the night. Intricate wrought iron lanterns in the medieval style hang from the corners of buildings and arches that join buildings they cast shadows along the narrow alleyways. If you choose you can circumnavigate the high walls to take in the magnificent view across the Valtiberina plain towards Sansepolcro and picture in your minds eye, knights in shining armour charging across the plain, their lances before them, flags and emblems flapping, the battle in full swing; the sound of metal against metal and the cries of men carried on the wind. The mighty Milanese finally defeated by the Florentines. It has been said that Anghiari, is one of the most beautifully preserved medieval towns in Italy.

We had often stayed in the three star 'Hotel Meridiana', a family owned hotel since 1964, situated opposite the 17$^{th}$ century theatre in the *Piazza IV Novembre* it is surrounded by ancient buildings and the lovely little private chapel once owned by Corsi family which is now a place of remembrance dedicated to the fallen of World War one. If you manage to get the right hotel room you could awake to the sight of row upon row of terracotta roofs spreading out at varying angles, interspersed with church steeples and medieval clock towers across the town. At night you can sit out on a roof terrace and just watch the world go by.

The owners of the hotel are wonderfully friendly and relaxed; it is spacious, clean and has a lovely restaurant in the basement. We would reserve a room over the Internet advising them of the date and approximate time of arrival, which always tended to be late in the evening due to our flight schedules. On most occasions we would arrive in the middle of the night but the sliding door always allowed us to enter a reception area that was invariably in total darkness. With no one present to check us in, hesitantly we would examine the booking ledger for a vacant room preferably with a view overlooking the town; take a key from one of the pigeonholes and retire for the remainder of the night. I would write a note in my basic Italian telling them which room we had selected. This custom continued for months during our frequent visits to see builders and architects and I often wondered why the furniture in the lounge beyond the check-in desk hadn't vanished in the hands of some dishonest opportunist during one of our arrival nights.

*

After leaving Bar Baldaccio and collecting all the paraphernalia associated with young children such as books, cuddly toys, wet-wipes and not forgetting the all-important coloured placemats, mementoes of our day out, we stopped briefly at the local park. The weather although by now a little overcast and with a gentle breeze, was positively tropical in comparison to the weather that Stephen and Angela were familiar with on the Isle of Man, where the sea mist could roll in at a moments notice and shroud the island in a dense fog. The park was empty and Chloe and Max had the run of all the play apparatus, the sounds of laughter and giggling filled the air as they willed us to push them higher and higher on the swings. After a few slips down the slide, a quick up and down on the seesaw we were back in the car and heading homeward, within ten minutes they were both fast asleep!

That evening I prepared a simple meal, meatballs in a *pesto* and cream sauce with a type of *pasta* called *Pappardelle*; it was quick and easy which meant I could spend more time with everyone rather than being chained to the cooker. Nick emptied the ashes from the wood burner, piled up the dry kindling, tucked in a couple of firelighters or *accendi di fuoco* and took a match to it, stacking the chestnut logs on top, it would soon remove the slight chill that filled the air in the Barn. In the height of summer, the thick stonewalls keep the rooms cool and comfortable while outside the temperatures soar; the coolness is a welcome relief.

We poured the wine and settled down to eat. The meal was soon polished off and after dessert it was time for a *digestive* or after dinner drink. We had bought a variety for Stephen and Angela to try, one of them Nick's favourite is *Grappa* a form of Italian brandy, he prefers the golden coloured *Grappa* to the crystal clear type. He finds it smoother and less harsh, the flavour apparently dependent on the type and quality of grape used in the distillation process. You can drink it neat or add it to an *espresso* to create a *café corretto*, which means a 'corrected coffee'. Me, well I dislike both types, just the aroma is enough to deter me and send a shiver down my spine. I prefer *Vin Santo or Vino Santo* meaning Holy wine it is a sweet amber coloured dessert wine traditional to Tuscany and is more akin to sherry. *Vin Santo* is commonplace on most restaurant menus. *Limoncello*, the syrupy lemon liqueur both Stephen and Angela had tasted on many occasions before, is very sweet and it is easy to forget that it is almost pure alcohol, that is until the following morning when you wish you hadn't liked it quite so much.

We had also bought a bottle of *Nocino* a strong yet smooth liqueur originally produced around the

Northern Italian town of Modena made from green un-ripened walnuts; it is a deep dark brown colour which reminds me of that disgusting syrupy cough mixture which your mum or dad always had to force you to drink when you were a child. Apparently *Nocino* is a great accompaniment to mature cheese or vanilla ice cream; this however remained to be seen. We have friends that own a property opposite two walnut trees, so if we liked it we thought we might have a go at making some the following year if they would be kind enough to let us have some of their walnuts. If following true tradition, the walnuts are supposed to be gathered on the 24th June, the 'night of *San Giovanni'* and when making it an odd number of nuts used. In Italy unlike England, pure alcohol is readily available over the counter, so *Nocino*, *Limoncello*, *Grappa* and other alcohol based drinks can easily be made at home and bottled; the Internet is awash with hundreds of recipes to choose from but here is one I have found.

*

### *Recipe for the liqueur Nocino*

1 Litre of 95% proof Alcohol
33 Green walnuts (approx 1 kilo)
1 Vanilla pod
800g of white sugar
Zest of one Lemon or Orange
1 Cinnamon stick

After washing and patting dry the un-ripened walnuts, cut them into quarters and place in a large glass jar (do not use a rubber seal) together with the sugar and stir. Leave for two days and then add the alcohol, stirring again. Move the glass jar to a well-lit windowsill and leave for sixty days, stirring the mixture every few days. After the sixty days have passed filter the liquid using some muslin cloth and decant into glass bottles and leave in a cool dark place.

The *Nocino* can be enjoyed immediately however true aficionados will let it sit for a year so that the flavour can intensify.

*

After much deliberation and replenishing of glasses a unanimous verdict was reached by all accept me, it was the *Grappa* that came out on top, closely followed by the *Vin Santo*. I only hoped that our heads were clear the following morning and would be able to survive the outing to the 'Goat Farm' that we had promised Chloe and Max.

The children were up bright and early and could hardly contain their excitement about seeing the goats. Fortunately none of the late night drinkers were feeling any the worse for wear after the impromptu 'liqueur tasting event'. If anything Stephen was keen to seek out some strong goat's cheese to accompany the *Nocino*.

The *Valle di Mezzo* or 'valley in the middle' goat farm is owned by an American man called Brent Zimmerman he has been running the seventy five acre farm at Toppole near Anghiari for nearly ten years. The farm shop sells a variety of goat's cheese, which you can sample before buying. Brent also offers tours of the farm, where you can visit the goats in the stables, see the dairy and learn about the various stages of production followed by the cheese tasting. Tours have to be booked in advance.

The narrow winding road climbed up and out of Anghiari for approximately ten kilometres until we spotted the sign that read *Formaggi di capra*. Luckily when we arrived the fifty plus goats were in their stables for their midday rest period having been out roaming the fields and forests for three to four hours. Away from the midday heat they stood in the coolness of the barn lazily chewing the cud and resting before being returned to the fields for the late afternoon feeding session. There were no fences or barriers on the farm and Brent has obtained consent for the animals to roam on neighbouring farmland although they are never unsupervised and always accompanied by BoBo the dog.

Chloe and Max dashed about the barn not knowing which goat to look at or stroke first, they were totally overwhelmed by these good natured animals who were not in the slightest bit put out by having children in their midst. Kids in all shapes and sizes ran about the stalls jumping about like spring lambs, bleating relentlessly for their mother's attention.

Goats apparently can be both stubborn and inquisitive and one such nanny goat was determined to use her mouth to explore anything that was within her reach. Having taken a fancy to Chloe's yellow sundress, Angela suddenly spotted the hem disappearing into its rotating jaws unbeknown to Chloe who was distracted by another cute youngster with its head protruding through the iron bars of its stall. Happily, Chloe's dress was removed from its mouth in one piece, albeit a little damp.

Having run out of steam and curiosity about goats the children were content to leave the animals behind and follow the cheese hunters to the farm shop where Brent met us. We were offered a number of cheeses to sample, some were fresh, and others quite mature. There were blue cheeses as well as the traditional classic goat's cheese called *Caprino* together with a type of Brie and a soft *Ricotta.* We were told that goat's cheese is good for your health and well being as it stimulates metabolism and also aids digestion. Stephen is no stranger to gastronomic delights having sampled some of the most extraordinary, even insect specimens from the Far East have passed his lips; these cheeses were tame by comparison. Nick and I were sitting down on a wooden bench, fascinated by the facial expressions that had become an entertainment. The two had selected yet another variety, this time a fresh soft cheese flavoured with red hot chilli peppers with an exceptionally strong kick, the initial shock to the system was almost palpable, but the smile of admiration for the skill of the cheese maker that followed said it all. Noses were seen to recoil at the most pungent smelling examples but they were also added to the list of purchases that began to accumulate on the counter.

Chloe by now was beginning to lose interest after so much fun so she jumped up on Nick's lap for a cuddle. Nick began to tickle her to the words of 'round and round the garden like teddy bear'… she giggled and squirmed, her legs waving in the air in a desperate attempt to contain herself, the words 'no granddad, no more' eventually escaped between giggles, but it was too late. It was not until Nick stood up to shake Brent's hand to thank him for the tour and the tasting that my eyes were drawn to a big round dark wet patch that was blossoming in the centre of Nick's cream coloured shorts. It was in the worst possible place its source no longer attributable to the overexcited four year old that had already left the room. Nick seeing the direction of my shocked expression looked downwards while the embarrassment spread quickly across his face. Brent could not have failed to notice as Nick quickly repositioned himself behind me.

"It must have been Chloe, when I was tickling her." But it was too late for explanations. "He must think I'm incontinent!"

"Granddad was tickling me." Chloe said to her mum who by now was beside herself laughing her socks off.

Back at the Barn it was time for Frisbee, football and hide and seek before dinner while Stephen and Angela enjoyed the last rays of sunlight with a book by the pool. Nick and I knew by the end of their stay we would be exhausted but the time would be over all too soon and we cherished every moment. Once they were showered and dressed ready for bed granddad was called to read the bedtime story, unable to finish before little eyelids closed over the memories of baby goats and little accidents that by the morning would be forgotten, but would granddad ever be able to show his face at the farm again?

With the chestnut shutters spread open in their recesses, brilliant sunlight burst through the windows and cast the shadow of the Roman bars on the herringboned terracotta tiles. This morning scene always reminded Nick of leaded lights in English country pubs, real ale and the ability to speak in his native tongue with strangers at the bar would be another pleasure that he was sure to miss. Although I knew his thoughts by the distant look he gave, he never said anything, at least not at the time.

During the winter months and the run up to summer, Nick and I always slept in what we called the loft bedroom, a smaller room that was warmed by rising heat from the wood burner below. The chimney, although enclosed passed through the bedroom giving off heat like a radiator. Chloe slept below us on a large sofa bed, Max still in a cot was with his mum and dad in the larger room. When Chloe, the first to wake, was up and about she would make her way quietly up the stairs and make us jump out of our skins and into another day of play, Max with the aid of an adult would follow soon after.

This day would start with an Easter treasure hunt; several small chocolate eggs had been placed in secret locations by Nick who had to slip unnoticed into the garden while the children ate their breakfast. Within reach of little outstretched hands in the low branches of trees, along fences and in dry stone walls the foil wrapped eggs in blues, reds and yellows glinted in the sunlight and gave hints and clues. Armed with plastic containers to collect their prizes they set off in different directions. All Nick had to do was to make sure that each found an equal number. I knew the pleasure of seeing those little faces light up was worth more to him than finding a chest of real treasure.

When the hunt was over, the decision was made as to how many eggs had to be saved until later and how many could be eaten; our peace and quiet was disturbed by the arrival of three elderly Italian gentlemen each with a wicker basket slung over their arm and a walking stick in their free hand. Some Italian conversation was required if only to discover what they were doing here and I was unceremoniously dragged out of the shower by Nick and told to get dressed.

"Hurry up!" he said as if something was on fire in the forest. On this occasion the three men wandered about the lower terraces of the garden with their heads bowed and their eyes fixed on the path they were treading, they were equally spaced like policemen seeking forensic evidence, picking about in the grass with their sticks. They continued chattering amongst themselves oblivious to the presence of two inquisitive, staring children and four mesmerised adults, one frantically trying to dry her hair with a towel while saying a polite *Buongiorno* to each stranger in turn. I was able to discover that the men were fungi hunters following a path from which there was obviously to be no deviation. I am sure that if they needed to come through the Barn they would have done so, completely unannounced.

The land around the Barn is littered with edible fungi of all shapes and sizes, but the edible are so similar in appearance to the deadly poisonous that without 'the knowledge' you are more likely to kill yourself or render yourself paralysed for the rest of your life. Nick and I had often thought about having a go at foraging for fungi ourselves and a friend of ours did ask her Italian neighbours if they would be willing to give us a few lessons, but they declined immediately. The locals know where and how to find the right varieties but are rarely willing to impart these jealously guarded secrets and would rather pretend not to understand what you are asking, than do so. All foragers have their own little patches, which they visit when climate and weather conditions dictate the likely presence of a recently arrived fungus. They know where and when to find them, it's almost like they possess of an extra sensory perception, and dare anybody else be in tune with the same fungi on the same day, all hell will let loose. Car tyres have been slashed if an unwritten law of territorial rights to fungi has been breached, and as we found out on the day of the treasure hunt, it doesn't matter to whom the land belongs. *Porcini* are big business here, like the *tartufi* (truffles) and woe betide anyone who gets in the way.

'The pocket guide to Fungi' book, I had bought for Nick the year before is very detailed although I will never be sufficiently confident to take on the task of identifying the ones we can eat.

"Why bother," he says "when the supermarkets do it for you. There's no need to go killing yourself over a piece of oversized mould." He's probably right, of course but I notice he always takes the book out when we go walking, keen to identify the ones that are marked with a double 'skull and crossed bone' symbol.

"Now this one has no known antidote," he says with mischievous eyes,

"It'll slowly rip out your stomach, destroy your liver and you'll be begging to die after a week of agony. Oh by the way" he continues "where have you hidden the life policies?"

I have been told that you can take your finds to a *farmacia* or pharmacy, where they will check the fungi for you; we however decided it was best left to the locals.

I managed to glean from the men that they were looking for a specific type of fungus called *Prungoli*. *Prungolo* (Calocybe gambosa) is quite a rare type of mushroom found only at this time of year. It has a festival named after it, the *Sagra del Prungolo*, which takes place in the nearby town of Pieve San Stefano during the first weekend in May. The festival promotes the regions local produce particularly food and wine. Italians don't seem to need an excuse for a festival, held as they are at regular intervals throughout the year; this one however is held at this time of year because it is the only time the *Prungoli* appears.

The men complimented us on the work we had done to the Chestnut Barn, in particular the garden since they were last here a year ago but they made the point with a stern look and a waggling finger of reproach, that mowing the grass does nothing for the *Prungoli*.

*

After the excitement of the chocolate egg treasure hunt it was getting more and more difficult to find things of interest to keep the children occupied. Max in particular wasn't in to hide and seek for any length of time, unlike Chloe who never seemed to run out of energy or interest. Max would kick a football about but he would soon lose interest and look for some other mischief to which he could more readily apply himself, preferably without being noticed. He did have a particular fascination with water, which meant he had to be constantly watched while in the vicinity of the swimming pool. The hosepipe was a major attraction and he would spend hours filling buckets and watering cans, then just throwing water about the garden, usually as close to granddad as possible. By adjusting the flow of water down to a trickle it wasn't difficult to keep this little two year old happy for hours. I have never seen such patience in such a young child as he watched the water rising slowly up to the point where he could still lift the bucket unaided and more importantly throw it over a considerable distance. I'm sure he'll want to be a fireman when he's older.

The hot warm weather had brought with it dry white roads and Stephen's hire car was almost unrecognisable under the deep layer of dust that had accumulated over the past few days. So it was that the fateful decision to wash the car was made before the heat of the midday sun made the bodywork more suitable for frying eggs. Armed with a bucket of warm water laced with that wash/wax liquid stuff and a large sponge Stephen unwound a long section of hosepipe from its reel and stretched it towards the car. The gun type attachment would allow him to rinse the foam away at regular intervals to prevent the car drying out streaky. After allowing Max the privilege of squirting water at the car in order to remove some of the dust the sponge was employed beginning with the driver's side and the roof, the foaming sponge rotated much to Max's fascination, this car washing lark was after all just a game. Realising he didn't have a sponge like daddy, Max disappeared inside to fetch his own in the shape of 'Bebe' his soft blue cuddly rabbit. He returned unnoticed on the passenger side and proceeded to rub the car door vigorously, unfortunately not with 'Bebe' but with a handful of gravel he had also collected on route. Don't ask me why the gravel because I have no idea but you can imagine daddy's horror as he progressed to the other side to find deep circular scratches that looped and swirled across the front passenger door. I know cars these days have few layers of paint but how Max had found the strength to get past the top coat and undercoat to the bear metal that was now glinting in the sun, I will never know. There is an important message in this tale and that is, no matter how careful you think you are going to be with your hire car the unexpected will inevitably happen when you least expect it.

If you have ever been to Italy you will not have failed to notice that there are two types of car, those that are immaculate and those that are not. Those that are not, usually look like they have just finished an 'old banger race' and lost; that is not so far from the truth as I will demonstrate. Car insurance is very expensive here and most people, particularly the very young drivers can only afford third party insurance. If you have an accident which is deemed to be your fault the insurance covers the cost of repairs to the other driver's vehicle but of course, not your own. Here it is the car that is insured, unlike in England where it is the owner or named driver. Repairs that are not covered are usually undertaken using a lump hammer and a crowbar, hence the 'not so immaculate' and these are the ones that seem to be so attracted, almost by powerful magnets to your pristine hire car. If you have driven in Rome or Paris you will know that its 'every man for himself' a bit like walking across a pedestrian crossing, and to avoid a collision in the chaos that usually ensues you must keep moving at the same pace as everyone else and avoid any hesitation.

Once Nick and I had the misfortune of having to use the road that circumnavigates the Coliseum in Rome on our way to the airport. It was just past midnight on Halloween and an impromptu car race was taking place involving mainly ageing Golf GTi's, every time we tried to get off at the exit we wanted we were blocked by one of the Italian 'boy racers' coming up on the outside who found the antic highly amusing. Cars chased each other while playing loud music and sounding their horns and we were caught out by a barrier of bumper-to-bumper GTi's. We had no alternative but to go round three times before Nick had perfected the right manoeuvre, breaking hard at the last minute while the trail of cars failed to stop and allowed us to escape, thankfully we still had plenty of time to get to the airport.

My first tip about hire cars is this, when they ask you if you want the excess waiver at extra cost agree to it, or better still take out one of those singular insurance policies that cover's the excess on every car you hire in a year. For as little as forty pounds it's worth it, just for the peace of mind. So when you collect your car and they say "sign here, here and here" on a form where the print is not only too small to read but is in Italian, all the while pointing in roughly the right direction while looking towards the ceiling of the office, you can relax in the knowledge that you won't have to pay the 1,000 euro excess for the new chip in the paintwork when you return it.

Nick and I once hired a car which after a few miles ejected it's gearbox on to the road, a replacement car arrived a few days later on the back of a tow truck, which then took the offending vehicle away, needless to say we were astonished to find a couple of months later that they had debited Nick's charge-card with over £800 to cover the costs, not only of the gearbox but the towing as well. A friend had a similar experience when he was charged for a rear parcel shelf, for a Lancia he hadn't actually hired. He now always takes a photograph of every vehicle he returns during 'out of hours' recording the time and date to avoid any attempt by the hire company making false claims against him. There are also stories of speeding fines being attributed to English hire company clients even though the offence was committed by another driver the day before their particular hire commenced. Be warned!

Whilst on the subject, speed cameras are a sore subject for Italian drivers, introduced as they have been in many places without warning and in locations often hidden behind direction signs or roadside shrubbery. It will come as no surprise that the Latin temperament is so often incensed to the point of vandalism. If not totally smashed out of recognition, camera lenses are all too often blackened with spray paint in the dead of the night. When the paint is removed by the State police the perpetrators return, again under cover of darkness to repeat the crime. All night vigils have failed to catch the culprits and it seems that even when the camera location is changed the process begins again. Drivers of more robust vehicles will bulldoze the poles on which they sit until the only picture the cameras are likely to capture is of a speeding aircraft. When the cameras were 'active', evidenced by an orange tint to the lens, a network of undercover spies from various impromptu action groups would immediately sound the alarm via mobile phone texts. As I write however there has been a temporary respite in these clandestine activities. It seems that neither the State nor the local *comune* can agree on which section of the complex Italian administration is to benefit from the fine revenue. The State has ordered the *comune* to pay for, maintain and operate the cameras and subsequently, collect the fines, forwarding the revenue to Rome. The *comune* was having none of it and all the cameras have now been inoperative for over two years and will remain so until the argument has been settled, if it ever is. But if roadside police with hand held camera guns ever catch you it pays to settle the fine as soon as possible, certainly within the specified timescale, as failing to pay a fine of one hundred and fifty euros will rapidly increase until it runs into thousands.

If the Italians don't approve of some new legislation or European directive, they will go out of their way to foil any attempt at it being imposed on them. You will remember the rubbish collection system in Italy, where bins of substantial dimensions sitting on wheels are located at various strategic positions along the roadside; an attempt was made recently to increase the refuse collection tax it resulted in hundreds of these bins mysteriously finding themselves in ditches or let loose on steep white roads. Roads were blocked with them and vast numbers were found on their sides in locations where it was almost impossible to recover them. We have even seen them in the middle of fields. How on earth the individual who was responsible managed to get it across the ditches we will never know.

# CHAPTER 7

At last Rover was fixed and ready for collection, good news because we had borrowed our friend Freya's Landrover Defender for longer than originally intended, a kindness typical of Freya who owns a beautiful Villa called Villa Michelangelo. Even though she is busy running a successful holiday business she makes time to lend a hand when it is needed. Set in an archetypical Tuscan landscape the main Villa is surrounded by five self contained apartments which overlook a heated salt water swimming pool; the white road approach is lined with cypress trees, its one of those roads that makes you wonder what's at the end. How she finds the time to arrange guided walking tours, fishing days and wine tasting excursions for her guests on top of everything else she does, I will never know.

Freya is one of those people that you would have no difficulty in describing as having a 'heart of gold' especially when it comes to animals. She has rescued dogs from miserable circumstances and taken in strays without a second thought, often finding them good homes. Once whilst returning from Florence along the lonely winding road through the mountains; a road that is not for the faint hearted, she came upon what appeared to be a weak sickly dog wandering aimlessly along; its head almost dragging on the floor. Alone, she stopped and the animal came towards her. She opened the boot and jokingly said 'hop in boy' and much to her amazement it did. Unfortunately Freya was not driving her usual vehicle which would have normally separated any canine passenger from the main interior by a mesh dog-guard. Every time she checked on the animal in her rear view mirror it returned her look with a penetrating and chilling stare. Her intention was to take it home, feed it up and find it a new home, as she had done on a number of occasions in the past. When she arrived at the Villa her own dogs came bounding up to greet her and upon noticing her companion their hair stood on end, their teeth were savagely bared and a defensive stance was immediately established. Freya managed to separate the dogs and return the newcomer to the boot of the car. The ensuing growling and barking alerted Freya's cleaning lady who came running to investigate what the commotion was about, she suddenly exclaimed *Mamma Mia, un Lupo, un Lupo*; Freya had inadvertently rescued a wolf. Fortunately it was in a relatively weak state and no real danger but that wouldn't have mattered to her, she would have done all in her power to save it whatever the situation. As it happened she gave it a much-needed feed and her son returned it to where it was found, a much happier young wolf restored to the wilderness. Now she has two pet wolves of her own, both magnificent animals and much loved by their owner.

That night whilst in bed we received a text message from Freya, she wrote with the sad news that Wayne had suddenly collapsed and had been taken into hospital. The diagnosis was distressing, a possible tumour on the brain, we were shocked beyond belief. I have to admit that being a lapsed

119

catholic I'm not one for regular prayers but that night I put my heart and soul into prayer, I lay awake most of the night struggling to come to terms with the news. The next day we contacted Wayne's wife Pamela and offered her our help and support. I knew from experience just how daunting it was to have your husband taken into hospital and I felt great sympathy for her. Despite being surrounded by marvellous friends all of whom would have turned out in support, there is no avoiding the loneliness and desolation you suddenly feel, especially when you have no idea how it will end. You feel totally helpless, a stranger in a foreign land, not only do you have the worry about your husbands wellbeing, but a multitude of other anxieties begin to snowball, making the ever present unwelcome thought even more difficult to subdue.

It's the small things that you wouldn't normally even consider that suddenly seem insurmountable. Driving alone on the opposite side of the road to the one you are used to is just one example. I was lucky, long before Nick became ill, I had deliberately accustomed myself to driving here and I knew the roads to Sansepolcro like the back of my hand. Wayne, to my knowledge had always driven their large estate car and now Pamela, more familiar with a small car suddenly found herself having to manage a regular trip to the hospital. Driving alone in an English car in Italy can be a disadvantage from the start, even before you encounter the less courteous, less attentive and seemingly less able Italian driver who creeps up on your tail like it is their intention to make some sort of coupling or towards you wanting your side of the road as well as their own. Pamela suddenly found herself having to drive the forty-minute journey to the city of Arezzo every day. This ancient city is beautiful but it is not one that I relish driving in. I would like to think that I'm fairly accustomed to the bedlam on wheels that is Arezzo at certain times of the day, but my heart went out to Pamela every time she made the trip.

For me there had been an even bigger hurdle, the language barrier, especially when it came to providing a medical history, the Italian doctors do not have the advantage of your comprehensive medical file built up over a lifetime. Here you have to start from the beginning and in Italian. It is also the patient's role to hold all of their medical records, including X-rays, which are often sent to your home in the form of compact discs, a practice that I had never heard of in England. Luckily for me I only had two sheets of paper to look after, notes relating to a fairly simple case of a blocked Saliva gland, whereas Nick after his time spent in hospital with numerous scans and tests had his own blue file!

Fortunately Pam was more proficient than I had been in making herself understood which when it comes to health issues is an important advantage. Unlike Nick, Wayne also spoke Italian so hopefully that would be one weight off her mind. I had hated leaving Nick every night alone in a ward full of strangers unable to converse. Factors such as your own wellbeing also tend to get pushed aside, regular meals or meals of any kind are no longer part of your daily routine. I dread to think what my mother would have said if she had seen the miniscule amount that I had eaten during those unforgettable and frightening eighteen days. I just hoped, with all my heart that Wayne would not have to stay in as long….

Now, when I think of dear Wayne my first thought goes to the very first time Nick and I met him. The Barn is, as I have already explained, situated on a huge flat area, rather like a ledge on one side of a mountain that cascades down to a deep valley below. It is in a forest, one kilometre from the village below and isolated; the expectation of visitors, let alone English speaking visitors was beyond imagination. At the time we were not aware of the fact that this easy-going gentle man wandered these hills and ancient groves around Fragaiolo following in the footsteps of St. Francis of Assisi. At times St Francis was alone when he travelled these paths eight hundred years ago, but Wayne had his companion, Rufus the Irish setter and on numerous occasions they had passed within yards of the Barn. This time they had taken the slight detour that brought them to our door. It was a sunny but cold winter day, when the man in the woolly hat, two walking sticks, red cheeks and beaming smile first appeared at the French window. It was an easy meeting as we chatted for well over an hour and shared a glass or two of red wine. Whilst the sun slipped beyond the hill, Wayne and Rufus warmed themselves by the wood burner we learnt that he was living his dream here in Italy his passion and enthusiasm for this beautiful country was almost palpable. The meeting was unexpected and in some way very comforting to know that an Englishman knew that we were here, I can't explain it any better than that. I guess Pam must have thought he had got lost!

Over the months that followed and into the warmth of the summer we met Wayne and Pamela socially and got to know them well. We had no idea of course that he had previously been diagnosed with a skin melanoma on his forearm, which had been removed several years ago. He had undergone regular checks and after five years had been given the all clear. Something had now sadly changed, and without knowing it at the time the prognosis was less than positive.

The Italian National health service is particularly good, we had discovered this from personal experience, and the care Nick had received had been exceptional. The technological equipment such as scanners, X-Ray machines etc., which are at their disposal in a relatively small local hospital, is beyond anything you might expect. There is even a cancer research and experimental establishment together with treatment centre at Bologna, which is just over two hours away, so knowing this and just how strong Wayne's faith was, I felt sure that if anyone could fight this, then he could.

*

The last few days of Stephen and Angela's holiday passed all too quickly and it was time to say goodbye, the quiet solitude they had left behind them was somehow cheerless, the mood tinged with sadness. Nick was finding jobs around the garden that had no real urgency and I felt his need for time to be alone with his own thoughts, it would pass in a few days of that I was sure. When you are free of the stresses of that nine to five existence you suddenly find that you have a little too much time on your hands, time to fill your mind with sombre thoughts. In the absence of the laughter and play that we would not enjoy again for many months, and the news about Wayne, it was difficult to raise our spirits above the gloom that had suddenly draped itself over us. In the days that followed we both immersed ourselves in the not so important tasks associated with living the dream. I made a list as long as your arm of things that I imagined needed to be done at the Chestnut Barn. The crisscross, ranch like chestnut fence which encircled the perimeter of the Barn and lawn was not desperately in need of staining and varnishing but it would save a job in the autumn. Whilst the paintbrush was wet, the gazebo and large garden shed would also fall foul of the dark chestnut colour that I had slapped indiscriminately about the place. Not knowing where Nick was I would ring an antique bell that hung from the *loggia* wall announcing a tea or coffee break, he would appear as if from nowhere, from some lonely woodland task, chainsaw in hand, hardhat on head sweat dripping into his eyes.

"That *ginestra* is getting out of hand." he had said and I knew it was a devil of a job to be rid of it. As pretty as it is in early May with its display of yellow flowers it spreads, ironically like wildfire, I say ironically because by mid summer it dries out and if accidentally ignited it burns like petrol. There was plenty of open space around the Barn, a swimming pool full of readily available water and a specially adapted valve that the *Vigili dei Fuoco* (Fire Service) could pump water from, if ever the need arose. There was also a large and powerful water connection within yards of the Barn, accompanied by nearly seventy-five metres of hose but we would take no chances. We had experienced forest fires near Sansepolcro and watched, fascinated as helicopters scooped water from the nearby lake of Montedoglio before flying the five or six kilometres to the heart of the fire. Huge containers suspended from cables would release their loads over the rapidly advancing flames, steam and smoke would rise into the air like a line of exploding bombs. We knew the risk of being surrounded by forest. During the summer months especially when the temperatures rise as high as forty degrees and the ground is baked hard, leaf litter, twigs and debris need only a spark and a breeze to establish a firestorm that will devastate acres of woodland in minutes. An army of emergency services is mobilised within an impressively short period of time, and in the aftermath the *Corpo Forestale*, *Carabinieri*, *Polizia di Stato* and almost every other official body you can imagine will try to find out how it started as we would very soon find out for ourselves.

Nick had trudged up the last stage of the track that led up from the village, much of which had been damaged by the winter rains and melting snow, the gouged trails through the gravel had left the approach to the Barn entirely unsuitable for normal motorcars. The moist air that sweeps along the Tiber Valley, across the plains of Anghiari invariably drops its load as soon as it touches the cold heights of Monte il Castello. Now it was time to fight back with fresh stone and gravel.

The air had that first promise of summer to it, and the flora, encouraged by the sharp and frequent downpours reminiscent of April in England, was bursting into life all around us. It too, would soon have to be forced into retreat by a two-week cycle of strimming and mowing. With renewed energy the sun would start to banish the pale grey reflection of winter, sun hats and factor 50 sun creams would be called upon by Nick and my olive skin would hopefully take on a new healthier sheen. Now we really would need a list and the fight against mother natures' attempt to claim back her lands, would begin in earnest.

We retrieved Rover from the garage and asked for the bill; both Ennio and Miranda had showed very little interest when it came to money so I asked them to email me with the figures. We had come to learn that the Italians were clever when it came to collecting money, for tax reasons their cash flow was often allowed to lapse, sometimes into the next tax year if it suited. Quite often a bill would arrive unexpectedly for something we had entirely forgotten about. Recently our *geometra* arriving at the local bank at the same time as us mentioned that an amount of 150 euros was due in relation to work he had completed for us some twelve months earlier. We had seen him on many occasions during the year but he had never mentioned it until now, and of course he preferred cash; his timing was impeccable I thought, as I stood there in the queue for the cash dispenser.

Partly with a view to road-testing Rover and with an urgent need to obtain gravel for the road we headed towards Pieve San Stefano and the quarry aptly named *Con cave* where you could buy various different types of rock and hardcore, as well as ready mixed concrete. The stone ranged in colour and dimension, starting from pea sized gravel to enormous boulders mainly used to shore up mountain landslides. White roads are made from a combination of fine, almost dust like particles and soft chalkstone lumps the size of the end of your thumb. When laid properly the dust and sandy particles bind with the stone to form a relatively smooth and robust surface. *Con cave* is a family run business and one of the brothers named Mauro had provided some resurfacing for us in the past. On that occasion he had arranged for a JCB digger to cut trenches into the hill above us to assist in channelling the water away from the northern aspect of the Barn and the steepest section of the track. On arriving at the quarry Mauro was out on a delivery and in my best Italian I tried to explain to the lady in the office exactly what was needed. After several minutes of misunderstanding I resorted to pointing and gesticulating. Eventually we had to venture outside and I pointed at the rough surface of the quarry entrance road and said *"per la strada"* for the road. In and out the office door we went weighing up the advantages and disadvantages of the various piles of stone and gravel scattered over several acres of open space, which resembled a miniature alpine landscape. There were gantries, massive cranes, a huge conveyor belt that must have been going on for one hundred metres in length, a vast range of heavy vehicles standing idle beneath silos, shoots and tubes of all sizes, a cement mixer that would have dwarfed the whole of our Barn. In fact it was like a scene from some science fiction or 'Mad Max' film, I found it just a little disconcerting, of course Nick loved it, "Bit different from B&Q this hey?"

I could see that she still had doubts in her mind, the long delays after each sentence suggested that she was awaiting a reply. My *non capisco* brought exasperated but good natured laughter and in the end, after some guess work on my part we had made a selection of sorts, at least that's what I thought had happened. All that was left now was to try and work out how much we needed. Some of the track near the barn would also benefit from a couple of reinforced concrete strips but how on earth was I going to explain that we also needed some steel mesh. In England when they say 'how many tons?' Nick would always say 'show me a ton' and we would go from there and they would deliver it in large bags that were swung from the back of the delivery lorry by a crane arm that grabbed the bags by the handles; the driver could manoeuvre that crane like a second limb. Here on the other hand they seem to do away with the nice wrapping, you chose what you need, work out roughly how much and the load is delivered and is tipped from the lorry, spreading itself out in the most inconvenient of positions. You then spend the next few days breaking your back moving it somewhere else. This would certainly be the case if the delivery lorry had difficulty getting in and out via the narrow track that led up to the Barn. Need I say more?

Back in the office Nick tried to draw a diagram of the width and length of the section of road that the water had washed away in March, he then tried to calculate a rough estimate of the tonnage. This of course degenerated into something of a farce when he went off with the office lady to look at lorries or more accurately at lorry capacities.

*"Due quattro per favore"* he was saying pointing at the lorry, I knew what he was getting at but I had visions of us ending up with two lots of four, i.e. eight loads which judging by the size of the lorry would have been enough to resurface a kilometre of track at least. He was struggling to say a half a lorry load and not knowing what a half was in Italian, thought he was telling her we needed two quarters. Well all I can say is I was delighted that she hadn't the faintest idea what was going on. I could tell by the deeply furrowed brow that this wasn't going well for her either when suddenly her expression turned to delight when the telephone rang and the large bell in the yard summoned her towards the office. The telephone conversation went on much longer than we

thought necessary, I'm sure after the initial few minutes she hadn't replaced the receiver and was busily talking to herself, deliberately trying to avoid us.

We were just about to leave when Mauro appeared. He greeted us warmly and after a few pleasantries we went through our requirements again. This time Mauro shook his head, raising his eyebrows and nodded his head towards the office door. Miraculously the telephone had been replaced on its stand and the office lady beamed relief at the return of her boss. He produced a pad and drew a diagram of a square metre and asked how many? We then followed him back to the yard he said

*"Penso che questa è molto meglio per la vostra strada"*. I think this is much better for your road. Simple when you know how!

The next day, cloud rolled down from the mountain and drifted in waves across our meadow masking everything in its wake. We stared out on the garden as if through opaque glass, it was difficult to see as far as your hand. Not a time for working with a chainsaw, fortunately we were having lunch with our dear friends David and Ernest so the weather was of little importance.

*

Citta Di Castello, the nearest English translation I can think of is Town of the Castle lies just south of the Tuscan/Umbrian border, it is the birthplace of Monica Bellucci one of Italy's most popular actresses who grew up in nearby San Giustino. She gave a magnificent performance in the film 'Under Suspicion' alongside Morgan Freeman and Gene Hackman. Other British celebrities are reported to have residences in the area. Angus Deayton is sometimes spotted in the *piazza* enjoying a morning coffee. The only celebrity we have ever come across was Hugh Grant who happened to be filming in Rome when we were visiting some years ago. Helen Mirren, I believe has a love for Italy and owns a Trulli in Puglia, southern Italy. Bill Gates, Maggie Smith, Mick Hucknall, George Clooney, Roger Moore and Sophia Loren are also among the long list of celebrities that own property here. Richard Branson has a hotel on the Amalfi coast in the beautiful little town called Ravallo. The town was made famous as the location for the 1953 film 'Beat the Devil' which starred Gina Lollobrigida, in her first English-speaking role with Humphrey Bogart and Peter Lorre. The film was financed by Bogart himself and directed by John Huston. Originally a box office flop it became a cult classic in latter years. Sting and Trudie Styler own a nine hundred acre estate with a beautiful 16th century Villa called *Il Palagio* near the town of Figline Valdarno just south of Florence, once the home of an Italian Duke.

*

Citta Di Castello is a delightful medieval walled city and a farmer's style market is held every Tuesday morning. When in residence, David and

Ernest visit the market frequently throughout the year. When we join them we lunch at a restaurant called *Le Logge* in the centre of the town. Arlind, who works the front of house, is always warm and welcoming and a circular table tucked away in the corner has become our regular spot. The restaurant is just off the main *piazza* and out of sight of much of the passing tourist trade. Mainly frequented by Italian businessmen and women during the day it offers very pleasant, tastefully restored and intimate surroundings under an ancient vaulted ceiling, it is ideal for that special evening meal. Arriving just after eleven o'clock we parked in the tree lined car park, which lies close to the huge stonewalls that once protected the town from invaders.

The walk of a few hundred metres to the pretty townhouse on *Via Borgo Farinaro* takes us past derelict ground that was once the home of two tobacco factories that have in recent years been demolished ready for redevelopment. The site was to be set-aside for a much needed car park, during the demolition however; engineers discovered the presence of a Roman aqueduct, mosaics and other treasures that would need examination by archaeologists. Work stopped some years ago and the ground has become rather unsightly with its orange plastic fencing now in disarray and in no position to prevent intruders. The *comune* examined the site of the second of the two factories and once again more mosaics were unearthed. Some experts believe that an amphitheatre dating from the 1st century AD once occupied the site. No further excavations have since taken place but it is believed to be an important discovery and I can only imagine that some dispute between developers and archaeologists continues behind closed doors. Already immersed in Italian bureaucracy, these valuable discoveries will likely be denied the waiting public for several more years to come. As you look to the left you can see a beautifully decorated arch and the *Palazzo Vitelli alla Cannoniera* that was originally built between 1521 and 1545 to celebrate the marriage of Alessandro Vitelli and Angela Rossi. The rich black sgraffiti style decoration that is present on the façade is the collaboration of the famous Arezzo born artist Giorgio Vasari and Cristofano Gherardi. The embellished walls overlook the formal symmetrical gardens, which were once famous throughout Europe for the exotic plants. In 1912 this beautiful palace under went restoration and since 1995 has played host as the Municipal Art Gallery. Paintings and sculptures by a variety of artists, together with a collection of bronzes by Bruno Bartoccini are housed in the twenty-one rooms dotted about the frescoed corridors and halls.

At David and Ernest's home we enjoyed the customary bottle of red wine usually a Montefalco, a pre-lunch ritual that was now firmly established as we caught up on the news from England. Being regular English diners at *Le Logge* our hosts had been given the task of translating a new *À la Carte Menu* into English. Arlind had given them a copy and with a little help from an Italian/English dictionary and even less help from me we completed the last touches before leaving for our much looked forward to lunch. The half-mile walk through the narrow flagstone streets is always special, particularly when the weather is being kind and the journey takes on the atmosphere of a leisurely stroll. Tall medieval buildings and *palazzi* dominate both sides of the *Corso Vittorio Emanuele*. Arched entrances that once allowed coaches to be drawn within are ornately decorated with prominent keystones above elaborate piers; a frame for the ancient and metal studded chestnut doors that now deny access to what lies beyond. In the walls you can see every aspect of centuries of change, bricked up lancet arches leave a trace of the architectural whim of a life lived centuries ago, recessed alcoves harbour the once vivid frescos of the Virgin Mother, that unmistakable look of concern still discernible despite the years and the storms that have since passed. Metal rings that once held the reins of noblemen's horses stud the walls, intricate and ornate; lion's head bronze doorknockers stand proud against the weathered and cracked grain of doors which have been repaired many times. High on the walls are the remains of the conical metal cages that once held the flaming torches that gave light. This is a town untouched by the ravages of time and of that conflict that scarred much of Italy and its people in 1944.

*Corso Vittorio Emanuele* opens out onto the expanse of *Piazza Matteotti* and *Piazza a Costa* dotted with restaurants and cafes, their colourful canopies harbouring the lunchtime trade. Designer shops and a plethora of banks occupy the quadrangle of medieval buildings as we cross and enter *Palazzo Bufalini* the 15<sup>th</sup> Century home of the aristocratic Marquis Giulio Buffalo. *Le Logge* occupies a corner within the palace's impressive and expansive arched courtyard or internal portico; towering above is an ornate glass and metal canopy, a masterpiece in itself that protects the beauty of the architecture from the elements.

Once seated within the restaurant you cannot fail to be impressed by the tasteful décor, stylish chrome and glass fluted wall lights stand out against the background of fresh white walls. Recessed alcoves hold wine cases, their lids askew with packaging falling out to reveal a tempting glimpse of a fine wine. The tables are laid with starched white tablecloths; the square plates are topped off with folded olive green linen napkins. Soft background music, barely audible above the ambience of the rapid yet soft Italian conversation creates a relaxed and friendly atmosphere. Smiles and greetings from already seated diners make you feel as if you are part of a select dining club, a privileged few who have discovered this hidden gem away from the main thoroughfare.

We selected our dishes from a set lunch menu; I deciding on the *Spaghetti Amatrica, spaghetti* with a spicy tomato sauce to start, followed by *Tacchino con limone e insalata*, turkey with lemon and salad; the desserts we would choose later. Whilst waiting for our dishes to arrive we chatted with Arlind as he browsed through the *À la Carte* translations. Once we had finished the first two courses of gastronomic delights it was time to select the desserts from the set menu, but Arlind had a surprise in store. Four assorted desserts arrived, obviously from the *A la Carte* menu, after sampling each we passed them around the table as discreetly as possible before giving our opinion on each. Later we would describe them more fully in the English version of the new menu, making them sound even more appealing, if that was possible. The impromptu game of pass the dessert consisted of dishes of warm chocolate cheesecake with cream and raspberry sorbet, apricot and biscuit mousse with a coffee cream flavoured sauce, what a delight!

A small glass of *Grappa* and an hours' conversation with our friends in the delightful surroundings of their town house, brought to an end another pleasant afternoon and it was time to return to the Barn.

*

Nearing home we made a deliberate detour along the narrow road that passes through the village of Colle di Fragaiolo where Wayne and Pamela had made their home. Wayne was looking a little drained of colour after enduring a gruelling course of treatment at Arezzo hospital, but he was nevertheless in good spirits. I felt that his positive outlook on this setback in his life would hold him in good stead to fight off whatever it was that had temporarily taken

136

hold. I selfishly wanted Wayne back to normal so that as soon as Nick had regained some of his walking agility after the accident, we could tap into Wayne's knowledge of these mountains and share some of the regular walks he had discovered since they had moved here. Poor Pam had also had a tough week, her strength and patience tested to the limit by one of those unexpected occurrences that always seem to add to your worries when you least need them. The clutch had gone on their car, right in the centre of Arezzo. Luckily there was a dealership on the outskirts of the city, so with the aid of the State Police she was able to have the car towed to them for repair. Arranging alternative transport after difficulties in getting her insurance company to provide a hire car, only served to exacerbate an already stressful situation.

We were greeted at the Barn with the loud sounds of Frankie the deer. We strolled up through the meadow to the gazebo to see if we could spot him in the field below, but to no avail, although his eerie bark continued to permeate the quiet of the early evening until well after dusk.

The spring and early summer warmth has its disadvantages as it brings unwanted guests in the form of the *zanzare*, mosquito's to you and me. The 'Tiger Mosquito' is a particularly nasty species, much larger than the common variety, it has a striped torso, hence the name. This one seems to want to make up for its winter fasting all in one go. Their breeding grounds are in the stream that runs through valley several metres below and how they can seek

137

you out from so far away is a mystery to me, but they do and when they do, you never know they have, until the next day. The lumps and bumps that appear in the most unexpected of places begin to itch, incessantly. So it was that we were delighted to be visited again by a most welcome guest, the mosquito's most fervent enemy, and our resident bat! During the summer months he spends his days hanging from the apex of the gazebo at the top of the meadow, as soon as darkness falls, he sweeps over the garden between his summerhouse and the Barn, gorging himself. He has the cutest little face, and visibly jumps each time I go up during the day to check on him, my few words of welcome startle him at first but he soon gets used to my eccentricities. Batty is one member of our Italian wildlife family that we want to encourage. Nick had read somewhere that a bat can eat up to one thousand mosquito's in an hour and he vowed that after finishing the essential jobs he would add 'bat boxes' to our list of things to do.

That night, exhausted after our wining and dining we retired to bed at an earlier hour than usual, it was probably just as well as our batteries needed recharging for the task that unexpectedly lay ahead. When you order materials as we had done, in this instance for the road, you never knew when to expect their arrival. The knock at the door at eight o'clock the following morning turned out to be Mauro from the quarry. I quickly pulled on my jogging bottoms and sweatshirt and scrambled, half asleep, down the chestnut staircase. There he stood, a warm smile on his face, waving an invoice and asking where we would like the six cubic metres of gravel unloaded. By this time Nick had joined me and together we walked down the lane trying to decide on a suitable spot. Our road being narrow and tree lined made it almost impossible for Mauro to manoeuvre the large ten tonne delivery truck piled high with stone and sitting on the top were two large strips of steel mesh. Eventually we agreed that the higher up the lane the better, so that when using the wheelbarrow to move the gravel we could use the slope to our advantage. After Mauro had leant the mesh against the nearest tree he pressed the button to complete the delivery process, hydraulics went into operation and the lorry tipped the load from the side. Kept in place by sheer weight the gravel failed to move until the load bay was almost at 45 degrees then with a crash like thunder the huge pile of stone cascaded on to the ground below. It wasn't until Mauro reversed his vehicle back down the lane that Nick and I realised that until we had shifted the mountain that we could barely see over, we were incarcerated, so there was no time to lose.

Redressed, in our shabby and well-worn working clothes we sat under the *loggia* drinking coffee, trying desperately to kick-start our motivation. The larder was running low and to refill it we would need to get Rover out so it was a job we couldn't put off. It wasn't until I mentioned that not only were we running short of supplies but that we had no wine in the house that my sluggish husband went off to collect the necessary tools. In a flash the shed was unlocked and armed with a shovel, pickaxe and wheelbarrow he'd set off at a gallop down the lane. Of course he had a plan that involved shovelling the gravel into the barrow, from the roadside out; the priority now was to get the road clear. Whilst this sounds simple, because of the size and weight of the gravel it took all Nick's efforts just to penetrate the great pile of stone. Eventually a routine was established and Nick brought the stone down the slope and deposited it on the worst areas of the track, whilst I raked it into the deep crevices channelled out by the torrents of water. Rover would play the part of the steamroller as soon as sufficient track was available to allow him to pass the pile.

It took most of the day to clear the track and repair the badly damaged areas, now we would concentrate on the reinforced strips on the steepest part of the track just before entering the gates to the Barn. Fortunately we still had the cement mixer or *betoneria* that we had borrowed from the builder in 2011, for a paving project; he had never returned to collect it. Apparently he has several such pieces of equipment scattered about the area and we surmised that until someone asked to borrow this one, it would remain here indefinitely. Once we manoeuvred it into position, connected it to the electricity the huge yellow drum burst into action quickly turning and shifting the mixture of sand and stone Nick had shovelled into it. Clouds of cement powder drifted like a fog on the breeze as he added a carefully measured amount of cement into the mixture. I was impressed, I had no idea what the mixture should be but he seemed to know what he was doing.

Pre-empting the need for the next ingredient I made a beeline for the hosepipe, which lay, on the other side of the swimming pool neatly on its reel. I ran back across the lawn, nozzle in hand, shouting the words "I'm on my way" when all of a sudden I was jerked backwards with some force. It was like being on the end of a bungee rope, losing my footing I ended up on the ground in an unsightly heap; the pipe had become snagged on the corner edge of the stone terrace. Much worse was the fact that I had inadvertently twisted the head of the hose before being forced to let go of it and now it was enthusiastically releasing water in all directions. The pressure from the pump is much higher than you would normally expect, as it has to be used to fight fires when necessary. Now it was twisting and wriggling, the nozzle rising and falling like a snake's head, unhappily towards Nick and the cement mixer. Nick was soon dancing around like a man possessed while trying to avoid the icy cold spray that seemed to be following his every move. I was not popular! Undertaking jobs that don't come naturally to either of us has been a source of consternation, frustration and laughter nearly always all at once, it's never boring and the laughter far outweighs the frustration. In the months that followed we would enjoy these memories on more than one occasion.

Nick by now was busy cutting the large metal grid into four long strips, once sunk into concrete they would be wide and strong enough to take any vehicle the final few yards of the steep incline, without churning up the gravel. The angle grinder screeched and whined its way through a quarter of an inch of steel as sparks flew off the cutting wheel making light work of resizing the metal mesh. We positioned the grid, emptied the contents of the cement mixer into the wheelbarrow and trudged on down the track. At the highest point of the section to be repaired we worked the bulky mixture into the channel Nick had laboriously carved out with the pickaxe. After filling in and stomping down to release trapped air bubbles we stood back to admire our handy-work. It would have to withstand temperatures as low as minus thirteen degrees during the winter months along with the torrents of rain water and snow melt that we had already become accustomed to; it had to last!

Our backs and limbs were already stiffening up and our enthusiasm waning, especially at the sight of an abundance of tools, which now lay scattered around the worksite. These needed to be collected and washed; then there was the mixer from which every last residue of cement had to be scrubbed and washed away. An hour later and barely able to walk upright we made our way indoors to the welcoming fire, which I had kept ticking over throughout the day. The thought of a hot shower, food and a soft chair to relax in, soon overrode the thought that we had to do it all over again tomorrow.

Our evenings' entertainment came from a laptop computer courtesy of the BBC and one of those inexpensive downloads that assigned a new UK VPN address, I think, but not being that technically minded I could be wrong. We had bought a HDMI cable, which linked our laptop to the television making the programmes easier to view via a much larger screen. It works well on programmes that have been previously aired in the UK; we only have problems when watching something that is 'live'. We had watched the 'Six Nations Rugby' the previous year but because of frequent streaming during the receiving process we are unable to boast of getting a truly live performance. Nick loves to watch the rugby and my mum who is also an avid Ireland supporter is often too quick to text the score, especially when Ireland is beating England, most disconcerting when there is a significant time delay. I have on many occasions had to sit straight-faced when the text alarm signal is raised. I dare not make eye contact with Nick who knows full well what she has in mind.

*

The following morning I awoke with the warmth of the sun on my face as it streamed through the bedroom window. Still feeling the effects of our previous days' labours I was determined to linger over breakfast until it became obvious that my enthusiasm for the long days work ahead had waned. Breakfast in Italy is generally a relaxed family affair as indeed is the case with most meals. Those that have an early start often break up the morning with breakfast at a bar somewhere on their travels.

Depending on where you are breakfast consists of some kind of regional sweet speciality or as they say here *Cornetto* and *Cappuccino*. In Piedmont breakfast is often comprised of *zabaione* which is a special cream made with eggs, sugar and *Marsala,* an alcohol not dissimilar to sherry. In Veneto an apple and raisin strudel, in Puglia toasted bread and ham, Calabrian's would almost certainly choose bread and spicy sausage. All these different specialities go hand in hand with the morning coffee, the Cappuccino that in its basic form is an *espresso* coffee topped up with warm milk. The word *cappuccino* is a derivative of the Italian word for hood or in Italian *cappuccio* relating to the hooded robes of the Capuchin order of monks and nuns who may have started the habit (forgive the pun) of adding milk to *espresso* coffee as early as the 17th century. By adding milk, the darkness of the *espresso* is transformed into a colour similar to the light brown robes they wear. The Italians however took the recipe to greater heights with the invention of the *espresso* coffee machine in the early 1900s. Now foaming steamed milk forms the top inch or so of the beverage and those that are particularly adept at making it, often decorate the top layer with intricate patterns forming heart or flower shapes, like the shamrock on a pint of Guinness, I have even seen the face of a cat staring up at me once. Cocoa powder or cream is sometimes added, depending on where you are in Italy.

Breakfast at the Chestnut Barn is not so elaborate, in fact facing apple strudel, *zabaione* with *Marsala*, or even toast and ham at daybreak is difficult to imagine, even *cappuccino* has so far failed to prevail over our fondness for English Tea an item that is often difficult to purchase here, even from the more accommodating supermarkets. Well, enough of my meandering through the delights of breakfast in Italy, it was time to start work.

By midday empty bags of cement lay strewn around the foot of the yellow cement mixer and the huge pile of gravel had been reduced to a small mound, once again the lane was clear and accessible up to a point. The cement would take at least a week to harden, so Rover was temporarily installed in a clearing in the forest and denied the confines of the chestnut boundary fence. Huge black beetles seemed to be attracted to the wet concrete for some reason and we spent what seemed like hours rescuing these delightful creatures, washing off the cement with a splash of water and carefully sending them on their way.

As we spend so much time out of doors it is impossible to ignore the fauna, seemingly curious butterflies passed within feet of us, some with the most astonishing colours and patterns on their wings. Some with tiny white wings with egg yolk yellow tips, known as 'orange tips', the much larger swallowtail butterflies drift in and out, sometimes they hover close by as if looking to see what we are doing.

The laughter like yaffle of woody our green woodpecker or *picchio* echoes around the forest in the valley below, his territory must now be well and truly marked, his cry a warning to any would be trespassers to keep clear; now all he needs is a mate. These are normally very shy birds but he is a regular visitor to the meadow above the Barn as he picks his way through the lengthening grass collecting insects, hopefully the biting kind. Our binoculars are always close at hand during the spring and summer months as there are so many curious animals and birds to watch. Woody, from April through to August, is in the habit of parading himself about the garden with a full plume of red feathers displayed on the top of his head. He is obviously trying to make himself even more handsome in the hope of attracting a girlfriend; apparently they chase their potential mate round and round a tree trunk during the mating ritual. They have a particular fondness for ants, eating up to two thousand a day. Ants are one species of insect we have more than our fair share of, almost every stone you overturn in the forest exposes a nest of these busy little creatures so we hoped woody would stay, set up home and over indulge himself. Large wood ants are black and measure up to a centimetre in length; they run along the boundary fence in both directions all day long. Nick is convinced they are eating it from the inside out because they seem to disappear somewhere within the larger posts and emerge in a totally different spot. They are impossible to get rid of without resorting to poison, something I am reluctant to use.

Turning over stones sometimes reveals scorpions, dark brown or almost black in colour, ranging in size from tiny to one and a half inches in length. These creatures are poisonous although their sting is not regarded as dangerous unless you are allergic to the toxin and suffer an anaphylactic shock, then you would need to seek urgent medical attention. Most sufferers carry an Epipen for just such emergencies. During the summer, especially when it looks like rain they get into the Barn, how they manage to is a mystery as most of the windows are covered with impenetrable insect netting and the doors are kept shut. I have had the misfortune of stepping on one during the night on the way to the toilet in bare feet, the sting penetrating my big toe. The effect is no more than an irritation that lasts for a day or two. Nick catches these little interlopers with a glass and a piece of card and places them a little way from the Barn, when caught they can be belligerent little devils and always put up a good fight. Nick says its good sport, but I'm not so sure. Once, when we were returning to England I unknowingly managed to pack one in our suitcase, as it survived the journey I was going to keep it alive and return it back to Italy but it died after I gave it a little tiny piece of cheese to eat. Not as silly as you might think, they eat almost anything although they favour insects and spiders, if they can catch them.

Reading all those travel magazines will never really prepare you for the things you might come across when you make the move to another country. Living amongst the wildlife we have, to some extent, become accustomed to new encounters and these experiences are generally welcome, the incredible beauty and diversity often awe inspiring, but not always. There would be lots of interesting new creatures to discover, some welcome at the Chestnut Barn others definitely not and inevitably the very thing that makes you recoil in horror is waiting just around the corner usually eager to share your living space, inside and out, as we would soon discover.

Just after three o'clock we called it a day, the task finally completed. I wandered about lethargically one hand cradling my lower back as I bent down to collect the discarded tools which lay strewn in all directions. Whilst avoiding the freshly laid concrete top section, Nick drove Rover up and down the lane to compact the new gravel; whether we had made a good job of it, only time would tell.

That evening as dusk fell the skies turned to that ominous dark blue grey colour that precedes a storm of significant magnitude. A deafening crash of thunder was just a second behind the flash of lightening and we knew that what was rolling over the top of Monte il Castello was about to discharge itself in the form of a cloudburst. Driving rain took turns with massive hailstones pounding the ground and roof; the sound began like a slow handclap and ended up as deafening applause. It lasted for well over an hour and there was nothing we could do but hope. When it stopped we couldn't bear to look.

# CHAPTER 8

Re-levelling the scars left by the storm would have to wait for another day because today was the day the *Mille Miglia Storica* car race passed through our town of Sansepolcro. Here we would congregate for lunch with friends at a local restaurant ideally located to provide the best view of the cars that take part, without even leaving our seats. Later we would enjoy the carnival atmosphere that prevails throughout the town and admire many of the classic cars that fill the towns car parks. It is here that the drivers and their co drivers will stop briefly for lunch before continuing south to Rome. It is an annual event held every May, although the route and towns where the procession stops for lunch can vary; the very first race began in 1927 although over the years the format has changed to prevent the accidents and deaths that have plagued the event over the years. Now it is less of a race and more of a parade of pre 1957 classic cars, traditionally only 375 cars are allowed to participate. The qualifying rules are strict, and to be able to take part, the cars must have either participated in the original race, have previously applied to take part, or be a car of sporting history listed in the Palmares winners list of international significance, the car must have been manufactured between 1927 and 1957.

The cost of entering is over 7000 euros per car, which includes hotel accommodation on route. The race takes place over two days and begins at Brescia in Northern Italy travelling down the east coast towards Rome; there is a final return dash from Rome up the west coast back to Brescia. In recent years the race has been preceded by 140 Ferrari owners who pay homage to the classic cars by leaving a few minutes before their historic counterparts, providing the thousands of enthusiasts that throng the route, with an absolutely unmissable spectacle. The Ferraris' that participate fall into two categories, 'classic' for cars built between 1958 and 1984; and 'others' for those built between 1984 and the present day. Many a celebrity or sports personality can be seen. Last year Nick and I had seen Clive Woodward the England Rugby coach, this year Daniel Day Lewis and Chris Hoy were competing in 1950's Jaguar sports cars.

Sansepolcro lies forty minutes away from the Chestnut Barn, on the plains of the Upper Tiber and at the foot of the last stretch of the Apennine Mountains. The area was historically populated by the Etruscans and then succeeded by the Romans; the fertile plains once covered in walnut trees, provided a source of timber to both. 'Birtugia', a Roman camp was built on the spot where Sansepolcro now lies and a number of Roman summer villas were built in the surrounding hills, one for 'Pliny the younger' who often praised the climate and the health of the native people.

The City, which has a population of just over sixteen thousand people, is probably best known today for being the birthplace of the famous painter Piero della Francesca (1416-1492). The memory of the great master is preserved in the *Palazzo della*

150

*Residenza* or Civic Museum, which was constructed, in the 13th and 14th centuries. Its highlights include two of Piero's most important works, *La Resurrezione* and *La Madonna della Misericordia.*

As you enter the historic town through *Porta Fiorentina*, the only surviving gate of the four, and proceed straight ahead you will be drawn through the network of intersecting medieval stone streets, which lead towards the heart of the town, the *Piazza Torre di Berta.* The *piazza*, which now plays host to the many festivals and markets, takes its name from the tower, which once stood there. The tower was the symbol of the town as depicted in many guidebooks and on postcards during the 19th and 20th centuries. Unfortunately the retreating Nazi Army who detonated explosives within the ground floor destroyed it during the night of the 30/31st July 1944. The blast, which was considered at the time to be totally unjustified in terms of military operation, was intended to destroy not only the tower, but also the entire area and buildings which surrounded it. These included the Cathedral, the Bishops Palace, the Municipal Palace and the Court. Fortunately none of these buildings were damaged and the beautiful *duomo* or cathedral just off the main square, dedicated to San Giovanni Evangelista, now houses many beautiful works of art, the most important being *Il Volto Santo* an unusual carved wooden Crucifix of Carolingian origin, made from a single walnut log dating between the 8th and 9th centuries. Next to the Cathedral, is the 16th century *Palazzo delle Laudi* or palace of praises, it is now the town hall and houses a beautiful interior courtyard, designed by the local architect Antonio Cantagallina. A large portal embellishes the façade of the *palazzo*.

At the end of *Via Aggiunti* lies the Medici fortress, which was originally built in the 13$^{th}$ century, commissioned by Cosimo I de'Medici. In the 1800's the fortress with its angular bastions was transformed into a farm and it is now privately owned.

Sansepolcro is filled with many treasures within the museums, churches, convents and monasteries of which there are far too many to mention. Many are tucked away in the narrow back streets, out of sight of the main thoroughfare that is lined with designer boutiques and cafes.

Nicks birthday on the 20$^{th}$ May provided us with a very good excuse not to work but to take a trip out. We had never really made the time to visit one of the most important religious establishments in history, *La Verna* the well-known sanctuary where millions of pilgrims pay their respects every year to St Francis of Assisi. It is also one of our friend Wayne's favourite places. He has read many books about St Francis and is something of an authority on the subject; his birthday falls on the same day of the month as the Italian patron saint, born over seven hundred and seventy years earlier. As the crow flies, *La Verna* is only five kilometres north of the Chestnut Barn but winding mountain roads mean an eighteen kilometre drive through a number of mountain passes, hairpin bends and steep climbs which takes thirty minutes. To compensate the views are remarkable, the peace and tranquillity is almost tangible. You enter the *Parco Naturale delle Foreste Casentinesi, Monte Faltrona, Campigna*, which was established on the 12<sup>th</sup> of July 1993 to preserve the thirty six thousand hectares of natural environment. *La Verna* sits on the southern tip of this park that spans two sides of the Apennine mountain range between Tuscany and Emilia Romagna.

The surrounding hills are full of marked trails that crisscross the mountains; some follow the original route that St Francis himself had taken all those years ago. The sign posts mark, not the distance to *La Verna* but the time that it should take to walk there in hours and minutes along well-trodden cleared paths.

After parking the car the approach on foot is along old grey flagstones that lead you to the entrance gates of the sanctuary. Just outside the elaborate iron gates stands a large bronze statue of St Francis asking a small boy to release back into the wild the Turtledoves he was taking to market. Above you, exceptionally tall beech trees provide a vast canopy that protects you from the heat of the sun as you climb the final few metres. On entering the gates of this beautiful sanctuary, it's surrounding forest and rocky outcrops I defy anyone not to immediately sense the spirituality of the place.

We followed a small coach party of visitors, who with guidebooks in hand and ruck-sacs slung over their shoulders filled the path ahead of us. The tap-tapping sound of their walking sticks hitting the stone floor could barely be heard above the excited chatter until suddenly the sounds turned to hushed whispers as the revered holy sight came into view.

The Sanctuary is made up of a number of buildings, chapels, beautiful cloisters, gardens and walkways. Count Orlando Cattani of Chiusi della Verna gave *La Verna* to St. Francis in 1213 as a place for quiet prayer and contemplation. Five years later the Count funded the building of the first chapel *Santa Maria degli Angeli;* fittingly on his death the Count was buried in the chapel.

As you make your way through the 'Corridor of the Stigmata' that leads to the spot where St Francis received the stigmata in 1224, you can enter a small door on the right and find yourself amongst the vibrant lime green fronds of ferns that grow out of the constantly wet rock formations. The unmistakable sound of dripping water echoes through the low entrance to a cave, where St Francis often slept, and a metal grate now protects the horizontal stone he used for a bed. The huge sheer stone cavern was a cold and damp place even during the month of May.

The frescoes that line the 'Corridor of the Stigmata' were painted more recently between 1929 and 1963 and have subsequently been restored; they depict significant episodes in the Saint's life. Vibrantly coloured life size figures tell his incredible riches to rags story, the miracles he performed, the suffering he endured and his iconic love for animals.

The 'Chapel of the Stigmata' now stands on the spot where St Francis is said to have received Christ's wounds on his own body. The building was erected in 1263 under the direction of Count Simone da Battifolle. The famous Florentine born artist Andrea Della Robbia created the altarpiece. A glazed terracotta panel, which depicts the Crucifixion, the border, filled with enamelled lemons. The artwork stands at six hundred centimetres by four hundred and fifty, the largest he ever made. It was here in this Chapel that I took a moment of reflection from our sightseeing and prayed that our friend Wayne would soon be well again.

In the 'Chapel of Relics' within the main Basilica you will find St Francis's cowl and habit. The much-treasured relics of his garments were kept in Florence for nearly eight hundred years, and were returned to *La Verna* in the year 2000. There are also other interesting artefacts on display, one is a piece of linen possibly stained with blood from the wound in St Francis's side.

A portico of nine arches dating from the 15th and 16th centuries surrounds the beautiful Basilica of Assumption from its square bell-tower or *campanile* to the start of the 'Corridor of the Stigmata'. On the wall on the right is a niche which houses a bronze by V.Rosognoli, which was given to *La Verna* in 1888 by Pope Leo XIII; it portrays the Crucified Christ embracing Saint Francis. Unfortunately it bears the scars of bomb splinters caused by the bombardments during 1944, which *La Verna* endured. The *campanile* that luckily survived was built between the years 1486-1490 and houses a double peal of bells that can be heard resounding through the woods and valley below on feast days. The Basilica of Assumption holds services throughout the day, some of which can be attended by the general public and there are also festivals held throughout the summer, this year, being the *XXVI Festival Internazionale di Musica D'Organo* which includes organists from England, Canada, New Zealand, Germany and America.

Leaving the Basilica you enter the main square or *Piazzale,* from here you can leave the confines of the Sanctuary and descend eastwards through the old entrance. A stone paved thoroughfare resembling an ancient Roman road leads steeply up from the valley below to the friary. Facing the gated entrance above a long wooden seat, the first resting-place of visiting pilgrims, is written in both Latin and Italian: '*Non est in toto sanctior orbe mons'* meaning 'there is in the whole world no mountain more holy'. This welcoming statement is consolation enough for the devoted followers of St Francis who had made the strenuous journey on foot.

Just walking around the Sanctuary is a wonderful experience in itself, the peace and tranquillity seems to seep out of the very walls. The views from the highest point of the complex are astounding. Stopping only briefly for a coffee in the large refectory Nick and I made our way down a steep flight of steps to the place where St Francis prayed, *sasso spico* which translated means 'projecting rock', an isolated spot beneath a large slab of stone which hangs ominously between the two moss lined walls of the deep cavern, it looks almost as if it could fall at any moment.

The cavern wall is covered in thousands of tiny *Taus*, T shaped crosses that have been gouged deep into the rock face. Signs confirm that this was the place that St Francis called 'the wounded mountain' where he came to pray because it was here in this deep cool and almost claustrophobic fissure in the huge rock formation that he felt closest to God

Moving away from the Sanctuary, we wandered through the forest and followed the signs for *La Penna* the rock pinnacle where on a clear day you can see three regions of Italy; Tuscany, Umbria and Le Marche. The dense forest was as peaceful and silent as the Basilica; a path led the way through the huge beech trees where the only sign of life was the two nuns that sat quietly in prayer by a small chapel situated in a clearing in the forest. This was the cell of Blessed Giovanni della Verna who died in 1322. The path continues until reaching *La Penna* where finally you can take in the vista that leaves you spellbound.

Before leaving this remarkable and spiritual place we visited the gift and souvenir shop within the main complex that was overflowing with mainly religious items; guide books in many languages tell the story of Saint Francis and the history of *La Verna*. A multitude of carved figures and wooden Taus line the displays, together with wines and honey made in the locality. There was a section filled with books on religion and the various teachings of St Francis for both adult readers and children alike.

Whatever your religious beliefs it is impossible not to be taken aback by the way this place affects you. Friends with no particular leaning towards Catholicism or even Christianity, for that matter have tried to describe the sensation of their first visit to this place. Wayne our dear friend seemed to have a particular affinity with St Francis and always said that it is a special place. Even Nick who follows the theory that no matter what you try to aspire to, there is always someone more than willing to 'steal the stabilisers off your bike', did not fail to be silenced by the spiritualism that engulfs this mountain. Me, well little did I know that *La Verna* would be the place where later in the year I would attend my first Mass and for once in my life lose that overwhelming feeling of guilt every time I attended or passed a church, a Catholic trait I believe?

A week passed and again Rover required the attention of Ennio, and for once the cause of the damage and blame lay entirely with me. The rear window mechanism had failed me, and the glass panel was stuck awkwardly outside of the rubber seal that prevented water from seeping into the car. An unusual design allowed the glass panel to slide down an inch or two out of the seal so that the door could be opened, similarly once the door was closed the automatic mechanism pushed the glass up into its seal. Why cars have to be so complicated these days I have no idea. Panicked into an attempt to save the situation, instead of opening the rear door again I flipped the switch that lowered the window from inside of the car and it dropped remarkably quickly, too quickly in fact. Now it would not slide back up or down but sat indecisively at half-mast. Pressing the internal switch only served to produce the most awful metallic grating sound imaginable; continuing to press finally resulted in the unmistakable sound of something snapping.

Nick removed the inner door panel and tried his hardest to repair the mechanism, but it was not to be. The cable that facilitated the rising movement of the glass panel via a pulley wheel looked more like a bottlebrush than a steel cable by the time I had finished with it. As the window did not shut correctly it meant that the rear door wouldn't either; I was not popular. The door and window mechanisms are somehow dependent on each other

159

and now the two parts would have to be replaced. Rover was beginning to spend more time at Ennio's garage than on the drive at the Barn. The clutch had also begun slipping a few days earlier and Rover was rapidly becoming our largest financial outgoing by far. Our only consolation was the fact that over the years we had practically replaced every moving part and pretty soon we would be able to say that we had almost rebuilt the thing! Deciding when to get rid of a car is always difficult, especially when you have just spent another fortune keeping it going.

Once again we scoured the Internet looking for parts; it is much cheaper to have them delivered from England than to purchase them in Italy. A clutch is a surprisingly heavy piece of engineering, but the lock and window parts fairly insignificant. The cost of the shipping came to a little over £50 but the savings overall were considerable. Mechanical labour by the hour is a quarter of the cost of English labour. The parts were delivered direct to Ennio's garage in a matter of days.

In the meantime Nick managed to secure the door to the rear seat anchors using cargo straps so that it wouldn't fly open when going over the many potholes found on most Italian roads. When it came to the glass panel he tried to secure it with American 'Gaffer Tape', the many strips of tape disguised to look more like tasteless additional trim than the makeshift repair it really was. There are two problems with 'Gaffer Tape', when exposed to extreme heat it loses its adhesive strength, similarly when it rains it turns into mushy strips, rather like fly paper, the more it rains the easier it slides. Of course you never find these things out until you've tried them, but once discovered, taking Rover out became an exercise in planning in itself. Parking had to be underground in order to avoid both failures but this was not always possible. On one occasion we left the Barn in beautiful sunshine to get the weekly shopping. The only supermarkets with underground parking were in Sansepolcro. When we left the Barn there was not a single cloud in the sky, on the return journey a weather front came from nowhere and the sky opened. Needless to say the tape slid slowly down the glass panel before streaming behind the car like a loose wedding ribbon. The glass eventually dropped irretrievably into the framework of the door itself, which was impossible to repair in the middle of what seemed at the time like a tropical storm. By the time we arrived back at the Barn a loaf of bread had fused with its paper bag resembling wallpaper paste and a bag of sugar had turned to syrup.

We must have used at least four rolls of tape whilst waiting for the parts to arrive from England. We would often be seen parked up on the side of the road, both of us clambering in the back, one holding a strip of tape the other trying to slide the glass panel back into place.

In the days that followed we remained at home in fear of dislodging the window and not wishing to put unnecessary strain on the clutch. The rear end of the car was draped in blue tarpaulin held in place with bungee cord, the hooks attached to the wheels and stretched across the roof in case another storm arrived.

There was little more we could do other than potter about in the garden weeding and generally tidying up. Another job that desperately needed doing and one that we always seem to put off is clearing out the garden shed; this time we were going to be as ruthless as possible throwing away all sorts of things which had not seen the light of day for some time. On entering however and to our dismay the shed had become home to a trail of huge wood ants. We had no idea where they were coming from and more importantly where they were going until I discovered an ominous pile of what looked like sawdust on the floor below one of the beams. The trail came in from the left hand side, traversed the beam and disappeared through a hole six feet above the neat little pile of sawdust. We looked on in horror as the procession continued in both directions without interruption; with a small hand brush he brushed a gap in the chain but undeterred, they closed the gap and went about their business as if nothing had happened. Nick who is opposed to killing anything was dumbstruck!

"The cheeky blighters they have millions of acres of woodland and they have to eat my shed and my fence".

That's not quite word for word, there were also a few unrepeatable expletives that I am not prepared to put into print; 'blighters' is my polite word not his! Unfortunately there were too many of them to consider any form of gentle persuasion to get them to move out, so we had to resort to copious amounts of ant powder, puffed into holes and scattered in all directions. Clouds of white dust covered the floor, the shelves and powder particles hung in the air for several minutes like a dense fog.

As we peered in waiting for the dust to settle we heard the sound of rustling coming from a large blue plastic bag, which I had used to wrap the garden furniture cushions in for the winter months. As I looked, the form and shape of the bag began to change as the occupant darted about looking for an escape route. To prevent Nick from entering and inhaling any of the ant powder as his lungs were left in a weakened state after the 'pink sky' incident, I crept in with a scarf covering my nose and mouth. I picked up the garden shears and tiptoed to the back of the shed where the bag lay and as I stood over it with my shears poised ready to make an entrance hole, he said,

"Now be careful you never know we could be dealing with a snake here".

I must admit I hadn't thought of that and the very word 'snake' brought me to an abrupt halt, I dropped the shears and ran towards the door at breakneck speed.

"Now what do I do?" I said.

"Use those", he said, pointing to a pair of tongs that were hanging from an old fire companion set that had been relegated to the shed.

"I don't think I can do this," I said, as I watched him move further away from the door. By now the dust had settled but I noticed he still wasn't intent on taking over. The thin blue plastic bag in the corner of the shed continued to display the presence of an intruder and after all the commotion it seemed even more anxious to be on its way. I grasped the tongs hoping to be able to grab the bag before whatever it was had managed to make an exit. Holding the bag at arms length the contents suddenly spilled out onto the wooden floor and small pieces of cushion stuffing exploded in all directions. I was now in full retreat and nearly knocked my reticent husband to the ground.

All of a sudden a *topo* or mouse was running towards us, we darted from side to side to give him a clear run, it did the same; finally it chose a different direction successfully making its escape and we breathed a sigh of relief. Another lesson had been learnt, if storing anything you value, always place it in sturdy plastic storage boxes.

Mice do seem to be larger in Italy they have bigger ears and sad looking eyes. We encountered our first Italian mouse inside the Chestnut Barn, how it managed to get in is unknown. Nick and I have learnt never to leave the doors open and only open those windows, which benefit from insect blinds.

We knew we had a mouse when we found incriminating evidence under the kitchen sink. In order to try and catch him we removed all the fascias boards below the kitchen cupboards, with a torch the two of us lay down on the terracotta floor and peered beneath the units, but there was nothing to see but a few cobwebs. Italians are quite ruthless when it comes to getting rid of vermin and some of their methods are not as humane as either Nick or I would have liked. One approach is to place a plastic tray filled with a thick deposit of the vilest glue like substance in a location regularly visited by the mouse. The idea is that the mouse runs across it and immediately gets stuck, the forward motion forces the mouse's nose into the substance and it suffocates over a period of time, very nasty way to go. The usual mousetraps are available but usually made with steel and much larger than I had seen before. I don't like the idea of such traps in case the animal is not killed outright but suffers the agony of losing a limb. The trouble is there is no easy way of getting rid of a mouse especially when it is as determined to stay, as you are for it to leave. This one was a particularly crafty little devil and would try my patience to the full before the problem was finally solved.

In the end we tried every one of the available contraptions. The first attempt at the gluey plastic tray resulted in disaster as the mouse somehow became aware of its purpose and managed to tip it up on its side. The glue escaped all over the floor tiles and became almost impossible to remove; I had to use a strong solution of silicone remover after all sorts of detergents failed miserably to remove it.

Next we tried the metal traps and having placed some of the smelliest sheep's cheese within each strategically placed device we sat back and waited with bated breath for the sound of the spring being dislodged. Having tested them several times before setting them we were in no doubt that we would hear the crash.

Sure enough as night fell the metallic sound of the mechanism forcing the trap to bounce off the ground, broke the silence. As Nick approached the side of the kitchen cupboard, hesitantly at first fearing what he might find, the mouse stuck his head around the corner and nonchalantly proceeded to eat the piece of cheese in full view. Several times the traps could be heard bouncing in the air with the full force of a spring that would probably be capable of removing a finger with little effort, but still the mouse managed to escape.

Nearly two weeks passed before we finally resorted to poison. Italians obviously appreciate the resourcefulness of the native Italian *topo* because they have poison disguised as *ravioli*, only the *pasta* parcels come in either vivid blue or red colours; perhaps Italian mice are colour blind. We placed these little parcels in all sorts of places, even on top of one of the bookcases; we then made a note of the total number and where they all were. The following morning when we checked, the only one that hadn't gone missing was the one on the bookcase.

We looked everywhere expecting to find a little dead mouse but no such luck, by then I had become less of an animal lover, we searched behind and under every piece of furniture but still there was no clue to its whereabouts. By lunchtime we had given up when all of a sudden there was a scurrying noise coming from the direction of our pale blue coloured sofa bed. The mouse had only set up home inside the mechanism you could hear the sound of its feet running along the metal frame.

Fortunately for me I had lived for most of my life in the country and the presence of mice never bothered me apart from being conscious of the amount of damage and contamination they can cause. The two cats we kept as pets would take care of the situation naturally, so to speak. I guess this is where and how I became impervious  to the furry little rodents.

Slowly I walked towards the sofa bed, the noise within the metal mechanism stopped and with one quick lift I tilted the frame backwards, all of a sudden the mouse leapt out and darted in behind the kitchen fascia boards. As I slowly lowered the sofa back down to the ground there underneath was the pile of blue and red *ravioli* parcels along with half of the integral mattress; it had been stockpiling them, not eating them, it was obviously more concerned with making a nest out of my now ruined mattress.

You might be surprised to learn that we never did find out what happened to our Supermouse; in the end we gave up on the *ravioli* parcels and threw them out together with the rather inhumane glue tray and metal traps. The unwelcome little gifts that it left behind ceased appearing and the scurrying noises stopped altogether. Supermouse had moved out.

*

167

We woke early to a glorious sunny day that nevertheless had a chill to it; the wind was coming from the east and during the night had brought with it a dusting of snow on the peaks of Monte Il Castello. There was a clear line several metres above us that defined a winter reluctant to depart from a summer eager to arrive.

Four Virginia Creepers having started to leaf, were clawing a path up towards the canvas canopy we had only yesterday repositioned on the top of the pergola poles, their delicate tendrils reminded me of gecko's feet, hanging on for support to the smooth poles of grey metal. Last year during April the plants had fallen victim to the changeable weather; their leaves, which had started as vibrant green and red had emerged from the late fall of snow as shrivelled brown husks. Within days they had eagerly begun the journey all over again as if determined to build their strength and get to the top as quickly as possible, in case winter decided to return.

That afternoon we had a call from Ennio asking us to bring the car in, the parts had arrived and he would begin work on the larger task of fitting the new clutch. He would repair the window and door mechanism once the most important mechanical work had been completed; I think Ennio had said that we could return in a couple of days.... On arrival at Ennio's Miranda's head popped up from under the bonnet of the old red Panda she was working on, she greeted us warmly; no doubt thinking here are that mad English couple again. Most of our Italian neighbours thought we were crazy for living half way up a mountain. But at the moment we were probably Miranda's and Ennio's best customers and the beaming smile reflected just that. They both loved the fact that we tried to converse with them in Italian and they could laugh at our obvious mistakes as if they had known us for years. Ennio drove Rover into a part of the building that looked more like a residential home than a garage and placed him on the ramp ready to start work. Miranda went to fetch her white panda from the back of the yard and Nick and I were delivered to our own door in a matter of minutes.

"See you in two days" she said as she left us isolated and alone with no transport on the mad couple's mountain...

The two mile return journey would take less than an hour on foot so without telephoning, as conversations over the telephone can lead to all sorts of complications, we set off down the hill to arrive on schedule. Work on replacing the clutch had been completed but unfortunately Ennio's leisurely pace had been interrupted several times by concerned motorists who had probably discovered some mysterious irregular engine noise. We had been here before as you know, these little interruptions usually involved an indepth discussion, a rummaging around on the floor, the opening and closing of bonnets and mutually furrowed brows before the diary was produced and an appointment made. In the depths of rural Tuscany you cannot influence the pace of how things are done; complaining will make no difference, which in some ways is part of its charm.

What was of more concern to me was how on earth he was able to remember which nut or bolt had been put back into place or which hadn't, after so many such interludes.

Looking under Rover there didn't appear to be any major bits left over even though the work on the door and rear window mechanisms had not yet started. Unconcerned, as we were assured that it would only be a matter of an hour before Rover was ready and not wishing to climb back up the hill, we decided to take a meander around the immediate vicinity. The road below the garage has a sign posted for *Il Vigno* an *agriturismo*. These establishments are popular with visitors to Italy offering comfortable accommodation within a working farm, vineyard or olive grove which would often be uneconomical were it not for the tourist trade; here you can experience something of the 'off the beaten track' Tuscany.

As we sauntered on up the road we came across a cluster of houses and small barns around a central cobbled courtyard, at one time the homes of farm workers and their families. Now many of the younger generation have moved to Florence and other large cities to find work so the old houses are largely unoccupied and falling into disrepair; all that is left is an ageing population, many having lived here since before the war. In the long untended grass amongst the scattering of poppies and buttercups are the remnants of a past age, an old cartwheel the central spindle rotting away leans against the handle of a rusty hand plough, both are barely visible above the grass seed heads that twist and turn in the light wind. Leaning against the wall of a barn is an ancient millstone; warn smooth after years of grinding corn or crushing olives. A water tap drips into a stone sink the green stain of the water trail clearly visible against the grey; chisel marks on the hand hewn stone are still visible after the centuries that have passed. In the corner stands a beautifully crafted iron cross and I can only imagine that it marks a spot of some sad significant event long passed in the annals of time. It is as if the families abandoned the place only yesterday.

The barking of a dog, sensing our approach makes me jump, disturbs the silence and overwhelms my train of thought, an elderly Italian man dressed in camouflage trousers and a thick sweater sits on one of the balconies above, gazing down at us as we turn the corner of the barn, I smile and shout, *Buongiorno* in an attempt to break the unnerving stare that has settled upon us, a low indecipherable mumble is returned almost as a question.

"Why do Italians have to stare like they do?" Says Nick, making more of a statement than the asking a question. He was right of course, they do, but I don't think any offence is intended, they just like to look...especially the men! I shrugged my shoulders. I guess this man in particular was unaccustomed to seeing people strolling by his front door, especially *stranieri* or strangers, which must have seemed even more curious.

The barking, now of several dogs increased in volume and I must admit to being a little fearful, as the sound grew closer.

"Oh perfect, don't tell me he's set the dogs on us?" Nick said, expecting at any minute to be surrounded by a pack of *Spinone*, an ancient breed of Italian gun dog not renowned for being aggressive but more inclined towards slobbering you to death. Our eyes darted towards the source of all the commotion, an open *cantina* door and out pounced what I now know to be a *Bolognese* a small stocky white woolly dog; its hair falls in loose ringlets. This dog was obviously the only one permitted by its owner to roam freely, larger dogs distinguished only by the deep gruff barks that emanated from the door, remained tethered, this one rolled over onto its back and  adopted the 'tickle my tummy' pose.

With our initial worries about being savaged unfounded we continued down the narrowing lane until reaching another barn, this one constructed entirely of disjointed timber from the boughs and trunks of ancient chestnut trees. The planked sides that must have been cut by hand had been fastened into position using square topped nails. The corners of each plank that curled outwards at the edges had been weathered into smooth rounded shapes and the whole structure took on a deep silver grey sheen that varied with the patterns created by the grain. It must have been hundreds of years old and now best described as 'rustic', a term, which suited its 'look' perfectly. There are many such barns in the forests and groves; in all shapes and sizes they were once used as shelters for the families who worked together during the harvesting of the chestnuts.

Leaving the tarmac road behind us we joined a rough track with deep ruts created during the wet winter. This was ankle-breaking country and I was anxious that Nick kept to the smooth grassy centre to avoid a repetition of the last accident; this was the only part of the track left intact. Extremely tall grasses, which reached my elbows, hampered our progress silvery green seed heads arched forward and embedded themselves in our clothing as we tried to make our way forward. The warm weather after such a wet spring season had created unusually strong and healthy grass, which was determined to spread its seed to pastures new, my cardigan providing the perfect vehicle. This once important road-link to the village of Valboncione was now no more than a narrow path leading through the overgrown verges following the river in the ravine below us. Overhanging chestnut leaves, still delicate and almost ethereal against the bright sunlight provided a canopy that kept us in dappled shade.

Opening out onto a clearing our mountain towered above us and we knew that the track would eventually take us through the village and on upwards towards the Barn. Long before the main roads were built this track was almost certainly one of the only ways of reaching the village without having to travel through Fragaiolo, cutting off a huge bend and saving a least a mile and a half of steep incline. We were finding our way around using the old donkey and ox-cart routes that wend their way through the chestnut and oaks over the mountain to Arezzo, Florence and beyond. Taking fattened animals, cut oak for the city fires and produce grown on these steep mountain foothills to market across the Apennines was common practice in the middle ages. Drovers and farm carters would sleep below the stars taking several days to reach the city markets.

Of course we had no intention of making the journey home yet, not without Rover but this little jaunt would stand us in good stead when we looked for the circular walking routes that would help build our lost fitness in the weeks that followed. We would turn back at the end of the village before the incline began. At this point the cobbled alleys and paths of Valboncione faded into the rough track that was the mountain pass that snaked its way up for eight hundred metres beyond the Barn before reaching the peak. Where the road meets the track, flat mountain rocks had been laid to form as near a smooth surface as possible, it put me in mind of the Roman road that runs past the ancient forum in Rome on its way to the Coliseum. How the stonemason could find so many huge pieces of stone to fit so perfectly was beyond imagination, I swear you wouldn't get a thread of cotton into the fissure that divided each one they were fitted so beautifully.

After checking the time we began our return journey back through the village, as we passed one of the few occupied houses a neighbour insisted on providing us with light refreshment and a tour of their house. These are people we had come to know well during our stay, although the conversation was held back by our lack of Italian the hospitality is an example of the friendliness and kindness of the local people.

Now running an hour later than intended, we arrived back at Ennio's garage, which would have stayed open until 8pm if it had been necessary. We collected Rover who for the time being at least, was in full working order.

\*

Two delicate crystals in the shape of a crescent moon and a single star hang from the chestnut lintels above the windows, a slight draft turns them gently and the colours of the rainbow that dance around the bedroom walls keep me mesmerised drifting in and out of sleep as the early morning hours pass. Nick is already up and about as he often is with the first glimpse of daylight, I can hear the distant sound of the scrub cutter attacking the brambles in one corner of the wood. House Martins circle above the shimmering water of the pool, taking it in turns to dive and scoop up single droplets, the air above is already heavy and filled with the insects that they will carry off to their young.

Soon I will ring the antique bell and we will sit in the sun over breakfast for an hour, before the work begins again. On days like this from midday till 3pm it is too hot to be working outside so we have taken to the Italian way of rising early and having a long break during the middle of the day before continuing with our labours until almost dark. Soon after dinner, sleep comes swiftly and the cycle begins again. Now the garden has lawns leading up to an Italian/English style wild flower meadow, with buttercups, oxeye daisies, cornflowers, cow parsley and long grasses that sway in the breeze, the only flower missing is the poppy. No matter how much we try to grow them by throwing thousands of seeds all over the place, the only spot they have established themselves is where we don't want them, in the gravel driveway. I can't bring myself to pull them up and so I have left them to their own devices and weed around them, their colour set against the deep chestnut brown fence and pale white gravel is a picture.

I wandered up towards the pergola at the top of the meadow, following the carefully mown path that Nick had cut in a loop to return to the Barn by another route, I had been keeping an eye on the tiny bat that had moved in amongst the timbers that formed the roof. Batty had been missing for a few days and I was concerned that the recently noticed presence of a multitude of owls had either driven him away or he had become a meal. I didn't know at the time that they change their roosting posts frequently during the summer months.

On one occasion when returning home after a late night out we had encountered an Eagle Owl perched on a post, its dark ear tufts and orange eyes suddenly appeared in the beam of Rovers headlamps, a ghostly spectacle when you have never seen the like before.

A little Internet research eventually identified the species and I can testify to the enormity of its stature. It was undoubtedly a magnificent bird, the largest owl in the world with a wingspan of up to six feet. Poor Batty, if he had encountered such a magnificent beast, he would have been a snack rather than a meal. The shrill tones of barn owls that ring out in the night, close to the Barn are nothing compared to the screech of the Eagle Owl.

*

The following morning our first job of the day was to replace the seal on the wood-burner that held the glass in place and prevented smoke escaping; now that summer had arrived we would not be need to light it for a while. We had noticed that on occasion when the winter winds came in gusts, smoke billowed from behind the glass panel. Having purchased a Carbon Monoxide detector some years earlier we knew nothing too harmful was being omitted, the high pitched bleep of the alarm never sounded and the digital reading only rarely registered a figure above zero. It was the one piece of equipment I would never be without when having to rely entirely on burning wood for heat. The fireproofing rope was easy enough to find in this region of Italy, wood and pellet burners being the most popular form of heating. Most ironmongers sell it on a reel where it can be bought in metres or cut to your required length.

We made our way down to the town of Pieve San Stefano to see Enzo the Ironmonger; he was married to an English woman and had learnt a smattering of the language, so we conversed in a mixture of both English and Italian on a regular basis, which was quite an interesting and amusing experience. When it came to describing DIY and household items Nick would point and offer the English word, Enzo the Italian equivalent and we would have a good laugh together.

Having turned off the main road we drove past the store where we buy our *Bombole*, gas cylinders for the hob at the Barn and followed the road that ran parallel to the River Tiber or *Fiume Tevere* which passes through the town some twenty feet below the road. The River Tiber flows for two hundred and fifty two miles before reaching the sea; it is the third largest river in Italy. It flows from the source of two springs on *Mount Fumaiolo* located on the border of Tuscany and Emilia Romagna. At the point where the river rises there is a marble Roman column topped with an eagle, which was erected by Benito Mussolini in the 1930's it is inscribed with the words '*Qui nasce il fiume sacro al destini di Roma*' which translates as 'Here is born the river sacred to the destinies of Rome'. Pieve San Stefano is the first populated area that the river reaches, although for the most of the year it is no more than a modest mountain stream. It is not until the river reaches the town of Orvieto in Umbria, further south that its volume increases as it makes it way down through the City of Rome and out into the Tyrrhenian Sea.

In the ironmongers after our usual pleasantries and our game of identify the object in English and Italian, we bought the fire retardant rope, some blacking paint to re-spray the front section of the burner and left. At home Nick carefully dismantled the glass door, which was secured in four places by steel plates held in position by short bolts and tightening nuts. Slowly and methodically he removed all of the holding nuts, bolts and plates and placed them in little plastic containers in the order in which they were removed. He wagged a finger at me and said,

"Never forget the five Ps".

"What's that? I said knowing full well that it would be some management speak he had learnt during his banking days. He pointed to the four plastic cups and said,

"Preparation Prevents Piss Poor Performance of course, didn't they teach you anything at school?"

"At school?" I said with a mock look of shock and continued watching as he proceeded to the next stage of the operation. He removed the old rope seal and cleaned the metal work with a wire brush and releasing oil. Varying grades of emery paper were to be used to affect a smooth surface,

"Grade two." he said holding out his hand,

"Grade one with a little water, please."

So it went on until he was finally satisfied with the result. He dried everything off with a cloth; to ensure that the surface would take the new adhesive rope he gave the whole thing a lengthy blast with the hair dryer. I stood over him passing the tools like a nurse

179

to a surgeon in the operating theatre. He gently handed the toughened glass panel to me for it to be cleaned thoroughly while the whole area was masked off with newspaper, in preparation for the re-spray. After covering our noses and mouths with surgical masks, the front of the wood-burner slowly took on the appearance of a completely new apparatus, as the special paint dried to a perfect matt finish.

The process of replacing everything went like a dream, each plastic cup gave up its precious content which went back into place without one single swear word, then a beaming smile of satisfaction spread across his face.

"Piece of cake." he said, as the glass suddenly slipped down by a centimetre.

"Not a problem, I'll just tighten this up."
With one turn of the nut the whole panel gave out an almighty crack, the so-called toughened glass had split from one corner to another. There was stunned silence before the onslaught of muffled alien words spilled from behind his surgical mask. I daren't speak my thoughts; I knew when it was best to keep silent as I waited for the tirade of unrepeatable words to subside. Now I could only think of the exploding glass shower screen which some may recall, took several weeks to replace.

"Not my favourite thing, glass is it?" he eventually managed. By now it was three o'clock and there was nothing we could do for at least an hour until Italy reopened its doors after siesta. My first plan was to contact the shop where we had purchased the two burners when we first bought the barn. We were regular customers after all, they must be able to help; we knew for a fact that they still stocked the same model as we had walked past it in their showroom many times. In Italy it is not as simple or as logical as you might expect. The shop situated in Pieve San Stefano was quite happy to sell you the burner but not it seems to provide replacement parts. The owner also had no idea where we would be able to find a new piece of glass, not that helpful at all in fact. Back in Rover we began to explore other possibilities and headed for Sansepolcro to a large shop called *Giornialdo* where again they stocked a large range of wood burning stoves and fires. Once again we drew a blank, here there was everything but the glass and after my various attempts to explain our dilemma the assistant directed me up the road to a glazier. This did not fill me with much confidence as we knew the glazier all too well, he had been the one who had helped us last year with the glass shower door and who had had to send the glass off for tempering somewhere in Perugia. What was supposed to take 5 days took weeks, deep down even I did not hold out much hope that he stocked toughened glass capable of withstanding high temperatures but I wasn't going to let on. Nick and I thanked the assistant, looked at each other blankly and left; Nick's frustration was clearly intensifying with every failed attempt.

"If I was in England I would know exactly where to go, save all this running around, here it's just impossible, it's an absolute nightmare; it'll no doubt be fifty euros for the glass and a full tank of diesel."

Always keen to fight the Italian corner I replied without hesitation,

"It'll be okay, if he can't help I'll find someone who can."

We pulled up outside the warehouse, entered and were greeted by the glazier who seemed to remember us from our previous visit, with the broken panel in hand I explained what had happened. Nick hovered by the door ready for a quick exit, he was obviously expecting the glazier to shake his head in response to my request but he simply walked over to a neatly stacked pile of glass, picked up the smallest piece and walked back to his workbench. He laid our piece of glass on the top of his, cut around it; he handed it to me and then asked if I wanted the old piece. My mouth still in the open position, stunned as I was by the speed and ease of his actions I couldn't answer immediately. This time Nick replaced the glass without incident, it had been a day that he would choose to forget, for me it was yet another obstacle that we had overcome.

# CHAPTER 9

Shutters and doors across the valley that have been closed all winter are suddenly flung open, fresh warm air dries out the damp musty corners of the summer homes of the many nationalities that have fallen in love with Tuscany. The villages have long since given up their young and ambitious to Florence, Siena and Rome. Once, land and property passed through the generations, but now old family homes have fallen victim to rising prices and in some cases, outsiders like us are welcomed in. The walls of these wonderful ancient stone buildings would simply tumble without new life; Italians don't want them. Many properties pass under Italian law to a multitude of family members and because they can't agree on what to do with them they just fall into the ruins that you see standing out like skeletal remains against the skyline. Over the past ten years empty and sad looking window boxes have become adorned with scarlet red geraniums or deep pink petunias, old traditional shutters have been replaced or restored, roofs reinstated using traditional materials or reclaimed weathered tiles. All of this activity has been carried out by people from all over the world under the watchful eye of the local *geometra,* anxious to ensure that Tuscan traditions will carry on well into the future. Most Italians have welcomed this wave of new blood flowing through Tuscany. Recently Russian buyers have added a new dimension to Tuscan life.

It is easy to make the mistake of becoming drawn to people of your own language for obvious reasons, whilst taking that step towards integration as difficult as it often is, it is essential, to become part of a community in order to enjoy the rewards that go with it. Many of the English and American friends we have made, have already become part of the community; their introductions have been an invaluable assistance in our endeavours to do the same.

During the late afternoon the whining sounds of grass strimmers and lawn mowers echo through the valley and voices are carried on the wind from the allotments and gardens that capitalise on the absence of chestnut and oak; it is a time for socialising with friends and family, being seen out and about at *passeggiata,* that famous Italian stroll designed to bring people together.

The following afternoon we had been asked to join some English friends for lunch, Yvonne is a wonderful cook and Robin the perfect gentleman and host. They love socialising and always have guests, Italian and English, coming to visit them during their summer stay. Their house is situated in a little *borgo* hamlet called Simonicchi, which is just across the valley to the North of the Chestnut Barn. A lovely walk through the forest as the crow flies may have taken an hour, but we would drive down through Fragaiolo, through Lama before negotiating the hairpin bends that climb pass the village of Salutio to Simonicchi and on to Chuisi Della Verna. The *borgo* consists of a cluster of stone houses some that date back to the sixteenth century. Sadly only one English Lady, an accomplished artist who lives alone and an Italian couple occupy two of the houses all year round; the remaining properties are second homes.

Yvonne and Robin spend the summer here, leaving during the month of October to make the long journey back to Britain. Robin had spent some years working and living in my favourite city, Rome and is therefore fluent in the Italian language. Yvonne goes to night school in London and can also speak Italian well. They have many Italian friends and when spending time with them I am able to practise my Italian vocabulary; one step at a time brings me nearer to my Italian roots.

A selection of cold meats, melon, *mozzarella*, tomatoes, pickles and olives make for an excellent and typically Italian lunch, maybe it is the sunshine that enhances all our senses or just the pace of life, time is a valuable commodity and here it often seems to be in abundance. Three hours later I am enriched with an multitude of new words that I am able to use in the correct tense. For Nick, I knew progress towards being fully absorbed into Italian life was going to take a little longer and I was ever hopeful that he would see the benefits of social gatherings such as these, but there were times when he sat in silence deep in his own thoughts on the outside of the circle around the table.

The following day, Chris an English friend and walking guide with a keen knowledge of this area was taking us on an excursion to some of the historic landmarks with a particular leaning towards wartime history. We had arranged to spend the day with him and his adorable Irish terrier, Seamus. Once in the car we headed north east beyond the town of Pieve San Stefano and up into the hills, passing the fields of ripening corn intermingled with scarlet red poppies to an area known as *Passo di Viamaggio,* Viamaggio's pass after the Latin *Via Maior* or main road. It is said that Julius Caesar settled a garrison by the pass of *Viamaggio* and more than likely stayed here whilst inspecting his troops. The road was an important link between the Roman Forts situated at Rimini and Arezzo. Caesar's lieutenant, Marc Anthony is also said to have been sent by his Emperor from this spot towards Arezzo with part of the Roman army to confront troops loyal to would be Emperor Pompeii. It was on days like this when walking and exploring that Wayne came into our thoughts, he would have loved to be able to join us on such an interesting walk and we just hoped there would come a day when he would be able to.

The family run hotel and restaurant called the *Imperatore* was our starting point we trekked through tall undergrowth on a narrow and well-trodden path, climbing higher as we went. The path ran along the top of a steep ridge, on one side the open landscape drifted in waves towards the valley that opened out on to the plain of Anghiari. On the other an oak and chestnut forest spread out in ever darkening shades of browns and lime greens until the denseness of the forest obscured our perspective. The woodland had been fenced off, probably in an attempt to keep the *cinghiale* at bay but judging by the deep furrows and churned up leaf litter everywhere we looked it had not been too successful. Chris led us in single file with Seamus in tow followed by me, Nick brought up the rear. I was never one to be the last in the line as I always allowed my imagination to run riot, the slightest sound behind me had me stumbling about as I checked to see what might be lurking in the undergrowth. Before setting out Chris had told us the story of his encounter with a wolf not so many miles away from where we were now. He and some friends had been walking and had come over the brow of a hill in the woods only to find a wolf stood in the middle of the path. The wolf undeterred, remained motionless it's eyes held firmly on Seamus, realising it was outnumbered or perhaps it just wasn't hungry, it eventually sauntered off in a rather indifferent manner. Nick and I longed to have a glimpse of one of these beautiful but very shy creatures but today we would only catch sight of the tail of a snake, very green and very quick as it slithered away towards the protection of the forest, non-venomous I think, or rather hope...

As we emerged from the dappled shade of the edge of the forest canopy into bright sunlight the landscape opened out in front of us, we were on the edge of an open field a vantage point retreating Nazi troops had used almost seventy years earlier to monitor allied troop movements. We stood on the ridge that looked directly south over the rolling hills towards Sansepolcro and beyond, we could see the unmistakable peaks of Monte Santa Maria in

Tiberina, Monterchi and Citerna. In 1944 the line of hills from which we now admired the most incredibly beautiful view had a more sinister purpose, known then as the Gothic Line, it cut Italy in half from east to west, and the concrete bunkers that are dotted along its length had been built using Italian slave labour. The ground still bore the scars of the ground-works that provided cover for the *Fascista,* a few Italian but largely Nazi troops who were desperately trying to halt the advancing divisions of the Allied armies.

*Lago di Montedoglio* reflecting the powder blue of the sky lay shimmering in the distance below us, the manmade lake that had slowly swallowed up the village of *Montedoglio* in the 1970s; then as the water took over the landscape, it finally settled in the shape of a crucifix. The plains of Sansepolcro lay beyond the lake and to the right nestled in the hills are the *frazione* or small villages, which are part of and make up the *comune di Anghiari* and the *comune di Caprese Michelangelo*.

It was difficult to leave this vantage point but after a short rest we made our way down a steep grassy mount known as Monte Verde and on to a pass which wound its way around the side of the mountain in the direction of Monte Macchione, this large steep cone shaped pinnacle looked for all the world as if it had been placed there by man. The climb in places was so steep we were forced to lean forward and use our hands to help steady our footing. After regular stops to allow our gasping breath to recover, we finally reached the top and there the magnificently engineered Gothic Line could clearly be seen. There were gun emplacements and deep bunkers that once housed machine and field guns, all linked by trenches and escape routes that led away to the north, a formidable fortress that had fiercely been fought over and sadly where young men had died. After so many years you had to use your imagination to visualise the bustling activity as the alarm was raised and men ran to their posts. Now covered in undergrowth as time and nature tries to obscure the legacy of a horrifying period of history, the scars still stand the test of time for all to see, a poignant reminder of those dreadful years.

If we were going to make it back to the start for a welcoming bite to eat we would have to get moving. Slowly and carefully we made our way down from the summit, Seamus was still as light on his feet as when he had started although the midday sun was now beginning to take its toll on the rest of us. We passed a huge white wind turbine, a modern and inharmonious addition to the beauty that lay around us. This towering monstrosity which marks the base of Monte Macchione can be seen from miles around from almost any direction, even from our gazebo in the meadow above the Barn, a focal point reminding us of this memorable day out.

As the terrain began to level out we took a shortcut through a field full of *Val di Chianina* cattle, these huge white beasts are renowned for the cut of beef served as *Bistecca Fiorentina*. At first these seemly placid animals took little notice of us until we came within fifty metres of a large metal feeding station that contained hay. It was then that they spotted Seamus and all at once heads and eyes turned in unison as the chewing and munching stopped abruptly. In their midst one beast stood head and shoulders above the rest; not being familiar with anything agricultural I was none the wiser and continued to walk at a leisurely pace. Nick however had worked in banking and had 'walked' many farms in England as part of his job.

"I think we should speed up a bit" he said looking in the direction of the herd, which was now taking a keener interest in us. The *Chianina* in the centre had taken a few steps forward and I can honestly say I have never seen such an enormous animal, except in the zoo. When I saw its rear, my mouth dropped open in shock as it suddenly dawned on me that we were looking at the father of all the cute little white calves that had taken refuge next to their mothers.

"Best not to panic" he says, breaking into a trot.
We cleared the gate at the bottom of the field like three soldiers on an assault course, then in the relative safety of the grass verge next to a main road, rolled about laughing, Seamus was totally oblivious, the bull, half way down the field had already considered us suitably seen off.

By now we had been walking for almost three hours, the heat was shimmering in the distance as it rose up like a mirage off the tarmac. The pace was quickening as the fear of the restaurant closing before we had arrived gave us a greater sense of purpose.

"See that bend up ahead?" Nick said, "Well that's

where the restaurant is, a cold beer and something to eat is waiting."

The bend looked at least half a mile away and by now even Seamus was beginning to flag and stopped to take a few minutes rest every time we reached the shade of an overhanging tree, he would not be moved until he was ready. When we reached the bend the restaurant was still nowhere to be seen, "See that next bend up ahe..." He tried to say, before I politely told him to shut up!

As we reached each twist in the road there was nothing to be seen beyond it but yet more road. Nick was behind me and could only gasp with exasperation as each turn failed to produce the oasis he was expecting, perspiration poured from beneath his sunhat but the continued rhythmic tap of his stick on the ground behind me told me he was keeping up with the pace. Half an hour later we had finally made it to the *Imperatore* restaurant and all three of us delighted in several long chilled drinks before devouring a well-deserved bowl of homemade *tagliatelle* with a *cinghiale* sauce.

*

Nick had been cleaning the swimming pool in readiness for the arrival of number of friends we had invited for a BBQ. It was another beautiful sunny day the heat only slightly moderated by an intermittent breeze. While I busied myself preparing salads, setting the table under the pergola and generally tidying up around the garden ready for their arrival at 12.30. Nick was occupied with reeling in the cleaning hose before beginning the process of flushing out the system. Before I go any further I should perhaps mention that in England you very rarely see snakes of any kind so it won't come as surprise to learn that Nick nearly jumped out of his skin to be confronted by one, close up. This particular one was probably getting on for a metre in length, black in colour with piercing orange eyes, a beautiful grass snake. When they met it was difficult to determine who was the most disturbed by the experience. I had no idea that snakes could move so fast, as I watched it turn tail and head off towards the forest.

It took a while for Nick to recover from the experience but with that said he set off stamping his feet and banging against the fence with the metal handle of the net, hoping that the snake had sensed his presence and was equally keen not to have another meeting.

We were never that sure if a certain snake was venomous or non venomous this being our first encounter. Here, those in the know say that if it doesn't move that quickly but curls up into a striking position, is fat rather than slim with a whip-like tail, has a diamond shaped head and a body with distinctive markings it can probably kill you if you don't receive urgent attention if bitten. Neither Nick nor I have the desire to find out. What we have learnt from the encounter is to be constantly on the lookout during the hot summer months; when walking out in the countryside or in the mountains, we make as much noise and general disturbance as possible. Even the normally placid grass snakes can become belligerent especially when they are in the middle of mating, that's what we were told by the local plumber/electrician when he too encountered a large grey grass snake when replacing a switch in the pump house of another client's property.

An hour later, with the BBQ fired up our guests began to arrive and the morning's unwelcome visitor was soon forgotten, barbequed meat accompanied by white and red wines went down well with my salads and grilled vegetables, cooked in olive oil and a splash of balsamic vinegar. For a time the conversation centred on aspects of living in Italy which I suppose is inevitable when so many of us are still getting accustomed to life here. Some of those present were better informed than others and some interesting new facts inevitably emerged. We were looking out over the mountain scenery discussing the vast diversity of tree species that stretched as far as our eyes could see, apart from the chestnuts and oaks that provided flour and heat to the local population there were large pockets of spruce and fir that stood out against an otherwise uniform backdrop. Apparently Benito Mussolini had been so impressed by the scenery of Bavaria when visiting his friend Adolf Hitler that he encouraged the planting of non-native fir trees in order to give the countryside a similar appearance.

Sometimes when you scratch beneath the surface of Italy you will find a deep routed admiration for Mussolini's legacy. When Nick spent time in the hospital at Sansepolcro he met a local Italian man and they built up something of a rapport being in opposite beds. Nick shared details of the conversation he had with this elderly and gentleman with the gathering at the Barn because on one occasion when Nick had expressed an interest in Italian history he was taken aback with what his new friend came out with, the gist of the conversation went like this:

"You won't like me then."

Anxious to find out why he should say such a thing Nick asked the obvious question to which he replied.

'When I was a young man during the war I was a member of the fascist youth, to me Mussolini saved Italy from becoming a communist country and he took a lot of the power away from the Catholic Church, he was my hero. You see?' he continued. 'This country was dominated by Catholic doctrine and the fear of the church was an integral part of the life of a suppressed people. Don't get me wrong, there's nothing wrong with religion but it doesn't mix well with politics. A lot of bad things have been attributed to Mussolini not all of it hearsay but there's no doubt he put the Catholic Church in its place, pushed the Mafia out of Italy and made the trains run on time as well. He brought the people together.'

It is also true to say that many Italians of this time were forced to leave their homes in fear of their lives, determined as he was to reform the country with the dictatorial will of an iron fist.

The trains still run on time, like clockwork in fact, quite literally to the minute. A paperback book is produced twice a year called an *Orario*, which can be purchased, from the newsstands or at the kiosks in railway stations. Inside it contains the details of every single train service that runs throughout the whole of Italy and it costs less than ten euros.

*Roma Moderna or Eur* (*Esposizione Universale di Roma*) was inspired by Mussolini; a suburb to the south of Rome, is a city within a city, built in 1935 it was intended to match the splendour of ancient Rome. Many of the buildings are decorated with carved stone murals depicting scenes from the evolution of fascism   and ornate Romanesque statues stand offering the fascist salute. The architecture is almost overbearing with its white marble halls that now house many government offices, separated by wide boulevards. Many Italians consider *Eur* to be a planning success, making it a popular area of the city to live.

Our conversation was still with Mussolini when I learnt of another city that he had built in the south of Italy called Sabaudia, a coastal city in the province of Latina in Lazio. Mussolini successfully reclaimed the Pontine Marshes, which at one time covered eight hundred square kilometres; where the likes of Julius Caesar and several subsequent Popes had failed. On this reclaimed land, often in the past referred to as the 'marshes of hell' he built Sabaudia probably the best of the many such towns he had created all over Italy. Work had been started in August 1933 and took only two hundred and fifty three days for the whole town to be complete.

Communist partisans shot Mussolini in 1945 his corpse was taken and buried in an unmarked grave in Musocco. He was exhumed on Easter Sunday a year later by neo-fascists; the body was kept in a trunk measuring one metre by sixty centimetres, and moved to a local convent before being taken to a monastery in Pavia. The police discovered the remains and kept them hidden for 10 years. His body was eventually returned to his family; in August 1957 it was entombed in the family vault at Predappio his birthplace, which lies southeast of Bologna and northeast of Florence. His tomb receives between 80,000 and 100,000 visitors each year and is still guarded by Italian 'black shirts' loyal to his memory. Several shops in the town sell fascist memorabilia everything from sinister truncheons, calendars and framed photographs. Many Italians would much rather forget this embarrassing phase in their history but others are determined to keep it alive as it is part of Italian life and culture.

At six o'clock the festivities began to take their toll and our guests started to leave. They always say that you should never mix the hop and the grape but Nick nearly always forgets these few words of wisdom once sufficient quantities of the same have found their way into his bloodstream. That is to say enough to dull the senses and the memories of those past painful mornings that usually follow such convivial afternoons and evenings. During the night he had woken with an overwhelming desire to re-hydrate with a pint of water and thereby prevent the hangover from hell that would invariably rise with him. So in the darkness he found his way to the refrigerator in search of the water we buy from the dispenser in the centre of Caprese Michelangelo. We now had four two and a half litre purpose made bottles with screw tops, which we regularly replenished with ice-cold *frizzante* (carbonated water) when passing the machine. There was also a large carton of orange juice in the fridge, which he mixed with the water, half and half; the added vitamin C could do nothing but good. I heard the clash of bottles as the door opened and then drifted back off to sleep and thought no more about it. An hour or two later I awoke to the same sound only louder this time, the fridge door slammed shut and I had visions of the contents being all over the inside of it when I went to look in the morning. On the return journey to the kitchen I heard the front door being opened and then shut and then silence for a few moments followed by frantic banging sufficient to wake our nearest neighbours more than a kilometre away.

"Where the devil do you think you're going?" I asked wondering if he'd suddenly taken to sleepwalking.

"I appear to have taken the wrong door; its dark at night isn't it? Ssssspecially up here….burp! Oops scuse me. The stars are lovely though."

Nothing more was said and he returned to bed and immediately resorted to snoring, a not unusual trait after a tiring day entertaining. The following morning I was up with the lark, the groaning coming from the other side of the bed had become too much to endure. Never one to stay in bed when the sun was shining, even if it only meant moving from the bedroom to a sun lounger on the terrace, I felt I was not wasting the day. Nick was slower to rise and when he did emerge it was immediately apparent that he was suffering with the pounding in his head.

"Didn't think I drank that much", he said opening the fridge door; "I do feel a bit rough. Where's that *frizzante* and orange juice?" He picked up the bottle and examined it through squinting eyes "Bit of a funny yellow colour this, you sure it's all right?"

As I opened the drapes that covered the French doors that led on to the terrace, the bottom swung out and caught one of the bottles which stood in the corner ready to be boxed up and taken to the glass bottle bin. This caused a domino effect and the whole collection toppled across the tiles like pins in a bowling alley, the chinking noise just about as subtle. The groan that emanated from the sore head with the accompanying look, spoke volumes.

"Not too good, hey?" I said as sympathetically as I could manage, not really expecting a reply.

"You don't intend drinking that at this time of the morning do you?" I continued, pointing at the bottle.

"Why is it off?" He says examining it more closely and shaking it as if it were a test-tube.

"Oh my God!" I said as the realisation dawned on me. "That's not water, its white wine. I decanted it from the box so that I could keep it cool in the fridge". I suddenly realised that it was a miracle he had woken up at all; he had been drinking pints of the stuff on top of everything else.

"That explains the midnight exploits in the garden". I said.

"What exploits? I don't remember anything." Came the reply.

# CHAPTER 10

We had no idea that dear Wayne was in such terrible trouble. A skin melanoma that had mysteriously appeared on his arm many years ago had been monitored on a regular basis and was, as far as Wayne and Pamela were aware, unlikely to cause any immediate problems. The tumour that had developed on his brain had been treated in Arezzo Hospital over a number of days and it had left Wayne in a weakened state from which we all hoped he would quickly recover. Although the prognosis was not as one would like we felt sure that if anyone had the will to overcome this setback, it would be Wayne.

We had seen him socially at a friend's BBQ, he was in a fighting mood determined to carry on as normal, dancing and laughing as if all was well, he seemed to be recovering albeit slowly. Out of the blue and within days, an infection had taken hold and he was rushed into the local hospital in Sansepolcro. To Nick and I this all too familiar place is one part of our Italian dream that we would rather forget. The lifts, the sterile corridors, that unmistakable smell of disinfectant, those signs that pointed towards scanners and X-Rays, plaster rooms, treatment bays and the coffee shop where I would sometimes find solace; I was all too well acquainted with. We passed doctors and nursing staff, cleaners and receptionists, people that we had come to know, a smile with a hint of recognition followed by a puzzled, over the shoulder look told me that we hadn't been entirely forgotten. Now I could stride purposefully down the long corridors no longer struggling to push a wheelchair up ramps, do three point turns to manoeuvre it into impossibly small openings.

At the nursing station we asked to see Wayne and were led to a quiet private ward. The transformation of the sleeping form that lay on the bed before us was a terrible shock. His face was pale and eyes that were half open seemed to drift in and out of consciousness. From the emaciated arms that lay still upon the bed covers emanated the needles and tubes that were there to fight off the infection. When he woke his words of welcome were slurred but the smile that passed slowly across his lips was unquestionably Wayne's. The conversation was light and we tried to offer words of encouragement, on the many occasions we had met him when he was out walking with Rufus we had asked him if we could join him as soon as Nick's ability to walk any distance had been re-established. This was a man that was fitter than anyone I knew. He had walked the hills so often that they had become like second nature to him and no better company would you find on the mountain if you encountered him.

"You have to get better Wayne, I had a metal detector for my birthday, and we'll do the battlefields together." I heard Nick say, but a fleeting look and a nod spoke volumes.

When Pamela arrived we left them in peace, it would be the last time we would ever see him alive, two days later he had passed away.

Pamela was incredible and obviously a lot stronger than any of us had given her credit for. She seemed to be operating as if on autopilot, arranging a funeral is difficult enough in England but in Italy there are so many obstacles that must be overcome but she coped admirably. Her two sons, Owen and David and other family members flew out to be by her side.

The funeral service was held in the small church of San Michele Arcangelo in Lama; the Mass presided over by Don Franco, the local priest. It was a lovely ceremony the music chosen was the hymn "Make me a Channel of your Peace" from the 'Voice of Assisi' by Friar Alessandro; the words ascribed to Wayne's favourite Saint, Saint Francis the man in who's footsteps Wayne had followed, up into the hills. As the anthem filled the church, a solitary butterfly fluttered over the coffin and then disappeared up into the nave.

Helen read 'A Time for Everything' (Ecclesiastes 3:1-8) in Italian and then Wayne's brother re read it in English, I thought yes "there is a time for everything if you make time, life is too short to put things off. Wayne lived his dream but it only lasted for three years."

# CHAPTER 11

As June drifted into July the mid-summer heat
intensified, thoughts turned once again to festival
time. Today was the 21st July; eight hundred years
ago Count Orlando Cattani had given St Francis the
mountain where he built his haven, *La Verna*. At five
o'clock within the walls of the sanctuary, drums and
trumpets would herald the arrival of the Count and
his lady; both dressed in finery that singled them out
as a cut above the rest. A procession of soldiers
armed with swords, shields and pikestaffs led the
way they fanned out along the path. Drummers and
trumpeters opened out in the square, their long
trumpets draped in the Counts colourful coat of
arms. There was not a single note out of tune or beat
out of rhythm. Children of all ages dressed for the
occasion, accompanied their parents. The pageantry
was extraordinary, the rich medieval velvets, silks
and satins in all shades of colour. Claret reds to cool

blues and soft lilacs, highly decorated with gold braids and embroidery, were a welcome contrast to the vibrant blue tunics and chain mail of the soldiers who lined the path that the dignitaries followed. The peasants dressed in sackcloth carrying wooden pitchforks and baskets brought up the rear. There weren't so many peasants as there were dignitaries I have to say. In contrast to the medieval atmosphere that these local people had created so well, the place also seemed to be dotted with *Carabinieri* and representatives of all the other police forces Italy has to offer. Waiting in the courtyard beneath the Basilica of Our Lady of the Assumption were the two wonderfully carved wooden thrones covered in deep red velvet. Once the famous flag throwers had finished impressing the crowds with their skills, which were sorely tested, when the skies darkened and the wind gathered strength; the count addressed the crowds.

We were there with our close friends Helen and Mick to watch the ceremony, then attend Mass afterwards. Helen, sings with the choir at *La Verna* at most of the special services held here, which I think is quite an accomplishment for a non-Italian. Although I was christened as a Catholic I had never attended a Mass and certainly not one on this scale, there were so many people. Nuns from every catholic denomination and all nationalities imaginable stretched out before me, dressed in habits of different shades of black, brown, grey and white.

Three Nuns from the order of Poor Clare's were seated in front of us. This particular denomination was a sister order to the Franciscans that was founded by St Francis's companion Clare. She was canonized in 1255 and her tomb can be found in the Basilica di Santa Chiara in Assisi. Both Francis and Clare had spent much time in the Church at San Damiano a sublime church set amid olive groves south of the *Porta Nuova* in Assisi, it is said that the reason why the church of San Damiano remains so authentic today is largely due to the faith and charity of a British family. Lord Rippon, a British Statesman and former viceroy of India, a dedicated convert to Catholicism, bought the church one hundred and sixty years ago just as the government were poised to nationalize it and expel its Friars. By buying and holding it in his name Lord Rippon was able to give the use of his private property to the Franciscans who were not allowed to own any property themselves. Lord Rippon also restored the convent. The ownership of San Damiano passed down through the generations until 1983 when its heir returned the church officially to the Friars with conditions that it was to remain unchanged forever preserving its spiritual purpose by welcoming worshippers to prayer with the friars in the old church and limiting the amount of tourist hours.

As more and more people entered, they bowed before the altar and crossed themselves in the traditional Catholic manner; there were people standing everywhere you looked, all deeply concentrating and listening faithfully to the words of the priest. If only my mum could see me now!

The Mass was in a mixture of Italian and Latin; therefore I had plenty of opportunity to just absorb the atmosphere. This is undoubtedly a beautiful church, consisting of a single nave with four cross-vaulted bays. Imagine, this building had stood here since 1509 and my mind wandered through those years trying to picture the congregation as they were then. The eaves filled with the sound of the responses and the singing by the choir was inspirational, this had been going on in this place for over five hundred years and very little had changed in all that time.

After communion the choir sang again, the main priest said the last prayers and concluded with the words '*La Messa è finite, andate in pace*' which translates to 'the Mass is ended go in peace', to which the congregation chanted in unison '*Rendiamo grazie a Dio*', 'Thanks be to God' and began to leave. It had been a wonderful experience one that I hoped repeat. Even Nick being more the conspiracy theorist than of any particular religious belief enjoyed the service; he was overwhelmed by the congregations' enthusiasm and obvious faith.

\*

After returning to Mick and Helen's we shared an impromptu supper made up of a variety of cheeses, crackers and homemade pickles which we polished off with the aid of four bottles of red wine, one of which is now a definite favourite and contender to

206

knock the *Rosso di Montefalco* from the pole position of Nicks favourites list. It is a wine called *Psyco* produced by a vineyard called *Villa La Ripa* which lies on the outskirts of Arezzo. The wine complimented the various cheeses of which most were produced from sheep's milk. *Pecorino Toscano,* which originates from the area around Siena, can be bought in various stages of maturity from a soft mild version to a strong hard textured and full flavoured type. In good company we hadn't noticed the hours flying by and as midnight approached we took our leave.

\*

It has to be said that we are not always up with the lark and the following morning was one of those mornings. The vast expanse of garden needed our attention however, so by ten o'clock we were up and about, although sluggish would be the word I would use to best describe our enthusiasm. The weeds were starting to take hold in the gravel driveway on one side of the barn. There is unfortunately no other way of dealing with them than getting up close and personal, so on hands and knees I slowly began the gruelling task. Nick was elsewhere strimming or mowing, I could hear the motor running and traced its movement up the paths to the meadow and beyond; I could tell the pace was slower than usual. I had noticed that the wildflower meadow was getting more and more established as the months went by. A new plant had turned up out of nowhere it seemed, but was now growing in abundance. It was not a plant that we had seeded when we began the meadow and I had never seen the likes of it in England. Tall stems competed with the grasses that stood half a metre in height, at the top of each the stems half a dozen delicate bell like flowers turned their heads towards the ground. The pale lilac colours became almost transparent in the sunlight. The flower was very like the 'Blue Bell' that grows in the shaded woodlands back in England but less succulent and probably hardier to be able to cope with the extremes of heat and lack of water.

There were patches of low lying Thyme in full flower, the clusters of beautiful shades of pink would give off a pungent appetising smell when Nick accidentally sliced one or two off with the strimmer. Golden Californian poppies that my dad had given me had returned and now stood out amid oxeye daises and cow parsley, while ferns in vibrant shades of green formed a natural border in the shade of the chestnuts and oaks that lined the meadow. There were interlopers of course, but the colours of the weakened bramble leaves added another dimension, turning as they shimmered in the breeze to reveal a darker shade of green in one second and silver in the next.

Butterflies in powder blue, white, orange and mottled shades of brown moved in zigzag patterns across this sea of colour and when one met another of the same species they would spiral upwards together into the sky. Along the borders the lavenders had bushed out and the flowers stood in strands above the leaves, a slight brush with the hand would produce that wonderful calming scent. Fantail butterflies in distinctive black and white colours competed with honeybees and hummingbird moths that seemed to hover motionless while waiting for a space. The only sounds came from birdsong, sharp and piercing above the droning of the insects and persistent chirping of the cicadas. The mowing had stopped; time to put the kettle on.

I seemed to spend hours weeding the gravel driveway at this time of year, but despite the constant attention it soon became covered with tufts of grass, clover and dandelions, only the most stubborn types of weeds seemed to find something to sink their roots into. It is a backbreaking job or knee breaking depending on how you approach it; the more parched the earth the harder the digging becomes. When the Chestnut Barn had been renovated the drive had been laid whilst we were in England. In hindsight the gravel layer should have been put down over a heavy duty membrane but for every negative there is always a positive as during this weedy season we also have an abundance of *fragole* wild strawberries that grow in the worst possible conditions, the village below us takes its name from this fruit, Fragaiolo.

As lovely as the plants are to look at with their subtle white flowers, during April to June the network of runners that each plant unleashes is remarkable and they are incredibly strong. Using conventional weed killer is not an option but I sometimes use a homemade, environmentally less harmful blend of white wine vinegar, washing up liquid and salt which you simply spray on, within a couple of days the plant is dead.

With late afternoon approaching we decided to drive to Anghiari to sample the inexpensive delights of Bar Baldaccio, having missed lunch, a *Pizza* or a burger and chips along with a beer and a glass of wine would see us through until the following morning. This bar is locally renowned for its *Pizze*, one of our friends has one named after him, 'Pizza Roger', the *pizza* topping that he specifically asked for from the most accommodating owners includes two fried eggs, olives and various other ingredients, when it arrived from the kitchen it was in the form of a happy smiling face just like Roger's. A small photograph of that very same *Pizza* now appears on the menu, a regular favourite even among Italian diners.

We passed the fields full of vibrant yellow sunflowers on the plain near Motina, the fields rotated annually between them, and the controversial tobacco plants.

An early night was called for so we set off for home at around seven o'clock the air was impossibly hot and although brisk winds moved it around there was no relief from the dry heat. With the air conditioning in Rover on full blast, we set off slowly back towards the Barn enjoying some of the scenery that we never seemed to tire of. To our right the Alpe della Luna had taken on the shades of dark blue and green, the heat haze between the foothills and the peak, made it stand out against the light blue of the sky. Cypress trees, stark and black in the haze and the occasional enflamed terracotta roof were the only signs of life; the sensible had taken cover in the coolness of their houses.

The valley plain was full of tractors and other farm vehicles that seemed to work around the clock to bring in the harvests that mature earlier here, progress towards home was inevitably slow but we were in no hurry. Up in front and away to our left we could see the line of hills that form the start of the Alpe di Catenaia range of mountains. The towering Monte il Castello and Monte Altuccia, the former no more than a few metres higher than the latter form the pinnacles of the whole range were clearly visible There was a slight mist just visible in wispy lines that rolled around and seemed to be caught in some sort of turbulence. I thought no more of it apart from thinking that mists at this time of year? They usually only followed a thunderstorm of considerable proportion, but there were no clouds anywhere to be seen.

After climbing up progressively towards the steep mound that was the old village of Caprese Michelangelo we began to descend the winding snake like pass towards Lama from this vantage point we would often look out across the valley to where Valboncione nestled into the mountainside and try to pinpoint the exact position of the Barn. We would even stop on occasion and follow the electricity pylons up from the village but to no avail, the Barn is surrounded by tall fir trees and is invisible from here.

The mist that I had seen earlier in our journey was now drifting down towards Lama, the fir trees that gave us our bearings and shielded the Barn from the winds that tore up the valley in winter, were totally obscured by its ghost-like presence. It suddenly dawned on me when I heard approaching sirens, we weren't looking at a mist at all; the whole of the side of the hill was engulfed in smoke. It was one of those occasions when your heart misses a beat; the Barn must be on fire. As we drove nearer we could see smoke rolling down the hill ahead of the flames that must have swept my dream away, behind it smouldering undergrowth marked the path of its destruction from the direction of our firs.

At the church the locals were gathered in the street pointing towards the thick grey smoke that continued to billow high into the beautiful azure coloured sky. We slowed and on opening my window one of the men shouted to us *Vai! vai!* Go! Go! The urgency in his voice and the expression of concern on his face left me in no doubt that he believed the Barn, to be no more. Nick also feared the worst and pushed the accelerator pedal to the floor, there was no time for pussy footing our way up the lane now. Rover bounced up and down, his suspension and shock absorbers taking the full impact, a trail of dust followed behind us.

After passing the ancient ruin of the Catholic Church, which sits perched on a pinnacle high above the lane, we turned the final bend to be confronted by a charred smouldering landscape. The *Vigili del fuoco,* the fire service together with the *Polizia di Stato,* the *Corpo Forestale* and the local *Carabinieri* were all there along with water tankers and fire engines of all shapes and sizes. We could go no further the final two hundred metres of our narrow track was blocked by the many vehicles that were there to deal with the emergency, a network of hoses fanned out from the assembly and disappeared into the forest. We drove Rover to a place of relative safety before walking back up the track. With a look of sheer panic on my face I tried to explain in broken Italian that we were the owners of the house at the top of the lane. We were allowed to proceed on foot, as we came nearer and nearer we could see the spot where the fire had started, no more than one hundred metres away. It was still smouldering wafts of smoke drifted from the undergrowth and away to the north; the fire had been blown away from us, the Barn had survived by the skin of its teeth!

213

Thanks to the local firemen aided by a natural firebreak in the form of an ancient track, which led to a chestnut grove, it was now under control. We still have no idea what caused this forest fire, perhaps a carelessly discarded cigarette thrown from the car by a passing woodcutter or the fragment of a glass bottle lying on the forest floor, which had caught the sun's rays and turned the place into an inferno. It was a mystery and one that was all too close for comfort.

The response from the emergency services in Italy is exceptional and we were impressed at how quickly they had managed to suppress a fire. Unfortunately however, as I have said before with every positive there is a negative and the repercussions from this incident were to be much farther reaching that we could have imagined...

Two weeks later we received a visit from the *Corpo Forestale*. Two very official looking policemen arrived in a khaki green Fiat Panda 4x4, their smart uniforms and peaked caps made all the more intimidating by the black handguns hanging from the holsters around their waists. Questions were asked and documents requested and we did our best to give our answers in confused broken Italian. Once the routine questioning was out of the way and they understood that we had been in Anghiari when the fire had started, they seemed to lose interest.

They obviously weren't quite finished with us as they then embarked on what appeared to be a tour of the garden, taking more than a passing interest in the gazebo at the top of the meadow, 'The Alamo' and our shed which had stood in its current position, not too far from the Barn for more than eight years. The question of planning consent suddenly came into the equation,

"Where did that come from, what's it got to do with them?" Nick asked when they were out of earshot.

I tried to explain to our visitors that we had asked our *geometra* if we could build a shed to accommodate all the garden and swimming pool equipment as we had no garage or *cantina* and he had told us that providing no cement was used then no permission was required. It was all about whether the building could be classified as temporary and the dividing line was the cement. All three structures stood either on metal pegs in the ground on a raft, nothing permanent about that, if Nick attached them by a towrope to Rover, I'm sure they would have moved to prove a point. There were a few 'your guess is as good as mine' gestures and before they left they said they would check their records, we heard no more for several days. This was, of course not unusual in Italy, as the wheels of bureaucracy are slow to turn; unless there is money owed to the authorities then it's quite surprising how quickly things happen.

Early one morning we received a knock at the door, and it was lucky we were up and dressed, as I don't think it was even 8am. There stood the local *comune* police officer with his English speaking assistant looking a little serious and after inviting them in we were promptly served with two official looking documents that had more writing and seals on them than the Magna Carta. We both had to acknowledge receipt of the said documents by signing the copy that bore our individual name.

The *Corpo Forestale* had indeed looked into the matter further and Italy, being as she is, in economic decline; a possible candidate for a euro bailout, needed extra revenue and unfortunately it looked like we were going to be the ones to help boost the coffers! We had ten days in which to make an appeal otherwise there would be an even heftier fine than the one they already intended to impose on us, for the 'criminal offence' of building structures without formal consent. I couldn't understand the wording but the part of the document that stood out was the figure of just over €5000, which I kept to myself for now. The policeman, Eraldo was as courteous as ever, he had come to know us over the past year and agreed that the structures posed no problem as far as the *comune* was concerned. The shed and the gazebo had been there since 2005 without one single eyebrow being raised by official visitors including Eraldo, who often hunted on our land. The *Corpo Forestale* who took precedence over any of the smaller forces, even the local authorities, was apparently enforcing the case; there was nothing they could do. Like us they too, were convinced that nobody would have been any the wiser, if it had not been for the forest fire. We sought legal advice and were told that building without planning consent in Italy was now a criminal offence and we should simply cut our losses and pay up. We were introduced to a member of the *Corpo Forestale,* by an English friend, he came to the Barn in an independent capacity, and said much the same thing adding, 'You cannot fight, they are too big.'

Later that morning we went to see our *geometra* and showed him the papers. This was the man who told us that we could build the structures in the first place; he looked at the documents and simply shrugged his shoulders telling us we would have to pay approximately €5000 in fines. He suggested obtaining the planning consents retrospectively, a further €1200, and then of course there would be his fee. There was no look of embarrassment, no word of apology or even regret. We were stunned, embroiled in bureaucracy and at a loss as to what to do. We spoke to friends, they agreed it was an outrage, they too were under the impression that no permissions were required if there were no cement foundations. We made a point of visiting a local carpenter who specialised in shed building; even he, a local Italian told us no permission was required. Armed with these facts we set about putting together a case and using an on-line software application translated our letter into Italian.

Fortunately we had taken photos all those years ago, showing the stages of construction of both the shed and the gazebo, so added these to the appeal document. Once complete we took it to the *comune* where they gave our copy an official stamp and passed the other duly stamped copy onto the relevant official.

We did not hear another word on the subject until weeks later when we received a notification advising us that the initial fine of €5000 had now been reduced to €516 euros which must be paid within fifteen days or it would increase with the passage of time. We had until the end of the month to ensure planning permission was in place. If this was not done they would demolish all of the buildings and bill us for the costs involved.

We went to the *comune* to ask if we could apply for planning permission for both the shed and 'The Alamo' the response was negative, only one could remain. To us there was no logic to their decision making process. 'The Alamo' that we had slaved over, dragging cut firs from the bottom wood for three weeks, hacking out the joints before roofing the whole structure, had to go. You could tell by the expressions on the faces of the two planning officials that they would not be moved on the subject and I could see that Nick was about to burst into a diatribe of all the reasons why we shouldn't be living here. So I simply said

"Ok" smiled, turned and left. Nick who I knew would be hopeless without me had no alternative but to follow. As we retreated the cavernous halls of officialdom echoed with the sounds of a very frustrated man, the swing door to the building closed behind me, the last English words I heard were,

"We have to face this everyday of our lives in this country…. Bloody bureaucratic bollocks…" I was at least content in the knowledge that they wouldn't understand what that meant.

At home 'The Alamo' was subjected to the chainsaw, and after an hour it and all the pent up anger and frustration, no longer existed but we had nowhere to store our wood for the winter.

*

With bitter resentment we reluctantly paid the fine and set about applying for the retrospective permissions. We had little alternative but to use the same *geometra*, to change now, and to start from scratch would not only be expensive but even more time consuming and time was a luxury we could ill afford. In any event I had no intention of paying him for his work, I still feel resentful over his mishandling of the affair and if he had been around when Nick had the chainsaw in his hand, well it doesn't bear thinking about. We had to get on with it, so we invited him up to take the necessary measurements for the plans and I gave Nick strict instructions to be nice.

We had actually known our *geometra* and his family for many years, so it was a little disconcerting that we had to sit around the table as if nothing had happened discussing a shed.

"We can add another three metres to the front of your existing building, if that helps." He said in rapid Italian, Nick looked at me expecting an immediate translation but I felt it best to pass this by. Ironically 'The Alamo' now just a stain on the ground was exactly three metres by two metres the exact same size as the extension he was now proposing. I had no idea if there was an Italian word for irony so I just nodded and said, "Yes please".

"You might as well." He said "After all you've paid for it already."

Too much advice I thought, Nick was still none the wiser and just smiled politely. I would tell Nick later when the heat had gone out of things and try and present this as a bit of a bonus.

"What are we to do with all the cut wood for the winter?" I asked, to which he replied,

"Cover the pile with the roofing sheets you took off the demolished building. Most people use plastic sacks, sheets of polythene, old corrugated iron, anything water proof, the *Corpo Forestale* don't have a problem with that."

I wanted to say, "So they don't have a problem with unsightly piles of rusty iron and rotting plastic sheets, but a beautifully constructed building that at the time of its demise was almost totally camouflaged by greenery and blended in well with a woodland environment, offends them does it?" But I didn't and Nick continued to smile when our *geometra* did and all was well with the Italian world that I was so desperate to stay in.

When the business of the day was finally over we sat under the pergola enjoying a drink. Our *geometra* had always described our Barn as 'a little piece of paradise', and he complimented us on how much work we had done in the garden and how beautiful it looked, it was nice of him to say so but it didn't help alleviate the negative feelings we were both feeling towards him at the time.

We chatted about Monte il Castello, the mountain opposite and he told us stories of the war. He told us that partisans were harboured in Valboncione as well as Caprese Michelangelo and that the Nazi's had held prisoners at gunpoint whilst they dug their own graves. It was difficult to imagine such atrocities in such a beautiful, tranquil place and it was during conversations like these that my mind often wandered to the family I never knew, my biological father, my grandfather and grandmother, what horrors had they seen and endured? My father may have been just a baby; an innocent bystander caught up in a cruel and bloody war.

When I told Nick later about the planning permission for the proposed extension to the shed he didn't take it too well, in fact he often took situations like this personally, believing that they made up the rules and fees as they went along, then immediately inflated them because you weren't born an Italian. He dictated a letter to the local Mayor and I translated it into Italian. He was young man in his mid-thirties and we had heard he was fair in his opinions and equitable in his dealings, so if anyone could help, he could and as in France he had the power to quash any fees if he felt them unjust.

The Mayor failed to respond to our plea, quite possibly the appeal letter had been intercepted and fallen into the hands of the planners so didn't reach the intended recipient. Episodes like these spoilt the dream, especially for Nick. I could cope with Italy's little idiosyncrasies but only time would tell if the scales would start to tip adversely for Nick...Unfortunately it wasn't going to end here as Nick, through no fault of his own would find himself in possession of an illegal firearm.

# CHAPTER 12

After the situation with the shed our spirits had hit a low spot and no amount of talking could make things easier. Nick was angry and felt as though he had been conned, he was probably right, unfortunately it takes a lifetime to get to grips with Italian bureaucracy and even then its seems one official has a different opinion to another. Still reeling after the fines, planning consent costs and what would remain in our minds as an incredibly unjust decision, the shed incident was high on our agenda of topics for discussion amongst the ex-pat community. At a BBQ we described what had happened, in the hope of warning any new acquaintances of the *comune* and *Corpo Forestale* ethics on planning. Mick, our host pointed to an enormous wooden structure that we could quite clearly see no more than two hundred metres away,

"See that over there?" He said "Well it's been there for some time now, the man who built it used to be a planning officer in Milan and when Eraldo was sent up to tell him to take it down; he quoted the exact chapter and verse of the planning laws and told him it was perfectly legal."

Not another word was heard.

It seemed to us then, that there was indeed one rule for them and another for non-Italians, either that or they hadn't heard of that particular law in Caprese Michelangelo. Anyway, it's in the past now and we have put it down to experience.

223

It was time to get out and about and try to re-establish positive feelings about living here, the weather and the beauty of our surroundings with a little history thrown for Nick's benefit, was a good place to start on the road to recovery. We were invited to join Chris, his long-standing friend John and Seamus the dog on another walk. The Nature Reserve of Monti Rognosi was to be our venue. Situated between Anghiari and Arezzo, at Ponte alla Piera this road follows the line of the river where when driving, your eyes are drawn to the deep blue of the rock that lines the narrow pass and glistens with each turn. From this pass we set out along a winding track that took us up into pine-covered mountains that rise almost vertically out of the deep gorge that is home to the river *Torrente Sovara.*

The reserve is covered in rare vegetation that survives directly because of the presence of the minerals found in the rocks formed from magma some two hundred million years ago. The rocks take on various different shades of colour depending on the type of mineral contained within. There are vivid greens; reds and violets that look like gigantic precious stones, sitting beside rocks of pure clean white and deep lustrous black. Iron, Silver and copper were extracted here from prehistoric time until the mid nineteenth century. Fifty years ago, farmers from the Tiber Valley smuggled tobacco grown on the flat plains near Anghiari up into the hills to a meeting point where it would be exchanged for gunpowder manufactured in Chitignano. The latter had been carried for twenty kilometres along narrow mountain tracks across *La Crocina*. At the meeting point, which was an old bridge, the swap would be made over a picnic lunch; the end of the transaction would be marked by the smoking of cigars made on the spot by the women of Chitignano.

Nowadays the area is a protected national reserve, home to many animals and birds, their likely location is marked by several information boards which also point out some of the hazards such as the regular presence of the more poisonous varieties of snake; we tread with caution. Wild flowers rarely seen anywhere else and the feather grass keep your eyes wandering in all directions; the air is filled with the fragrances of thyme and *Helichrysum italicum*, often called the curry plant because of the pungent smell of its leaves.

As we continued to climb, the views became more and more breathtaking, the narrow paths more treacherous and the terrain more wooded and steep. Much of this recognised walking route had been allowed to become overgrown and in places a machete would have been usefully employed. There was World War II evidence all around us as we traversed the Arno Line, the last Nazi defences before the Gothic line which we explored on our last walk. Tourist boards explained the history behind the defensive position and the circular rock formations that had protected machine guns facing the line of advance.

Seamus was by now beginning to flag in the tremendous heat and we decided that it would be best to head downwards towards the river where he would be able to cool off. I am not one to be keenly interested in animal droppings but during our descent we came across evidence of wolves, large dog-like droppings wrapped in what I will politely describe as fur coats were centred in the middle of the track. Its last meal was undoubtedly a small boar or deer, and a little disconcertingly the evidence was fresh.

The undergrowth began to thicken and soon we were surrounded by dense pockets of *ginestra*, the path almost blocked by the surge of growth that had taken place during the damp spring months. The path narrowed and soon we were following no more than animal tracks running snake like down towards the river. Our guide, having walked this mountain on a number of occasions warned us that some of these paths led towards precipitous cliffs. Having seen them from the road hundreds of feet below I was not keen to find out for myself so kept in line with Nick as usual bringing up the rear. After an hour we were looking down onto a flat-grassed area where rustic wooden seating was arranged in a semicircle, a clearing in the forest. It put me in mind of a scene from the cult film 'The Wicker Man' but it was intended for nothing more sinister than open-air concerts run by the local convent!

Ten minutes later John, Nick and I accompanied Seamus as he splashed about in the cool clear water, pawing at the pebbles, Chris had gone to collect the car, and I couldn't walk another step.

# CHAPTER 13

Sundays are traditional family and socialising days here and not wishing to be an exception to the rule Nick and I would be doing the same. Going out for lunch meant that you rarely returned home before early evening; there is something special about those long alfresco lunches in the warmth of the summer sun in the company of friends or family. It is not uncommon to find four generations of Italian family members sat around an extended dining table, from grandparents down to new-born babies. When you ring to make a table reservation rarely are you asked to give any specific time, normally you simply say whether it is for lunch or dinner, the table remains yours for as long as you want, there are no second or third sittings, the food and ambiance are there to be enjoyed at a relaxed pace….

*Il Capannino* is a much-favoured venue; a stunning *Agriturismo* immersed within thirty hectares of wonderful scenery and yet located only three kilometres from Pieve San Stefano, well out of earshot of the nearby busy trunk road the E45. We would be dining with our friends Helen, Mick and Colin; and a lady we had never met before called Patricia. Colin had also embarked on a complete change of lifestyle leaving behind the southern shores of England for a more favourable climate and stress free pace of life. He owns a part share in a big farmhouse with another Englishman called Anthony and Patricia's son, Luca. Colin stays here all year round while his co-partners divide their time between Italy, England and France.

It is always advisable to drive the *Spino Pass* to Pieve San Stefano slowly, the road seems to have more hairpin bends in it than the roads in the French Alps; travelling along it is not the best precursor to a pleasant lunch, taking its toll as it does on the hardiest of stomachs. Eventually we reached the town, passed through in the direction of Sansepolcro and climbed up the small white road, as we rounded the final bend the renovated farmhouse came into view. This large and beautiful building of almost white stone originates from the 1600's. It has been sympathetically restored externally using authentic materials preserving the characteristics of a traditional Tuscan farmhouse. Internally you are firmly in the 21$^{st}$ century, as you enter you are greeted by tasteful and expensive looking décor that radiates luxury from every corner. Aspects of the old building are preserved but there the similarity with the hardships of 17$^{th}$ Century subsistence farming ends. On the ground floor the comfortable reception area accommodates indulgent sofas where you can sit and enjoy a pre-lunch aperitif with *crostini*, typical Tuscan mouth-watering appetisers. On the first floor there are four accommodation suites equally tastefully and luxuriously furnished; each one completely different in bold striking and contrasting colours of green, red, yellow and peach, all designed by the owner who has an obvious flair and talent for interior design. The walls are garlanded with works of art from every conceivable medium, each canvas or board has been carefully chosen to fit comfortably within its surroundings; bronze busts and statues together with less conventional art work are everywhere to be admired. A lot has gone into making this establishment 'as good as it gets' and I haven't even mentioned the food yet.

Nick and I had eaten here before and have always enjoyed the company of Giuseppe and Paco and revel in the delights of Paco's cooking. The menu here is a little different to those seen in the multitude of Italian restaurants dotted about the area; it is more international, more adventurous. Paco adds a twist to the normal dishes served, and his creations never disappoint.

Colin and Patricia arrived, and after the introductions we embedded ourselves in the blue Renault plush sofas while chatting and enjoying a chilled glass of refreshing *Prosecco*. In the bottom of each champagne flute was a pink coloured ingredient attracting the effervescent bubbles at its base. I had not seen this before but later discovered that it was a few drops of *Aperol*, the rhubarb and bitter orange aperitif, mixed with some sugar and frozen in an ice cube tray, a great twist to the customary glass of *Prosecco* in both taste and decoration. Our host refilled our glasses several times before leading us to our table. The restaurant area once the stable block, is now a beautiful bright sunny room with overhead exposed chestnut beams, the walls ornamented in the same tasteful style. Circular blue and yellow Sicilian Majolica style chargers with which our table was laid were a beautiful addition to an already elegant setting, stylish even down to the water glasses.

Giuseppe and Paco had both worked in London for many years and Paco was at one time House Manager to the Duke and Duchess of Windsor when they lived in Paris. Paco even has a glass ashtray engraved with the initials of Wallis Simpson and Edward, and a tobacco pipe that once belonged to the abdicated King himself. The Duchess died in 1986, fourteen years after her husband.

My eyes were drawn to what looked like part of an ancient rustic wooden window frame in pale blue 'shabby chic' style, looking through it on a canvas was the painting of a young man, head drawn back almost to 90 degrees. There were no hands visible but balanced on his lips was a bottle in the last stages of being emptied. It hung on the wall near the kitchen door. I was so fascinated by this unusual piece of work I hadn't noticed the arrival of Giuseppe who was by now standing at the head of the table reeling off today's choice of starters. Every dish is cooked using fresh ingredients so the availability of dishes is dependent on the availability of seasonal produce. Catching the last two choices on Giuseppe's list I opted for the *frigiatelli con formaggio di capra*, sweet green peppers with goats cheese, whilst Nick, not so keen on goats cheese chose the *cipolle e pancetta crostata,* onion and bacon tart. For the main course upon realising there was only one portion of duck which Nick had already earmarked I was left with the either the mixed grill or rabbit *coniglio* the latter alternative which I must admit I tried years ago was not high on my list of favourites. The first course fortunately came and went slowly, giving us all time to savour each mouthful as well as the local red wine, which was decanted into rustic glazed terracotta pottery jugs, our glasses refilled so frequently we hardly knew how much we'd had.

All good things as they say must come to an end so after over indulging we declined a sweet and left, by now it was late into the afternoon and in order to prolong our enjoyment of such good company we decided to stop and treat ourselves to a *gelato* or ice cream from the *gelateria* in Pieve San Stefano. Row upon row of silver metal tubs line the chiller each one filled with ice creams of a vast range of flavours. Here we sat in our after lunch sleepy state to watch the world go by. It made me think of a news article, which I had read recently. Apparently Italians had banned ice-cream being eaten after midnight in the streets of certain districts in Milan. It was to prevent crowds of young people from gathering as the associated noise affected local residents. You were permitted to eat the ice-cream providing you remained inside the shop. Could only happen in Italy!

"Is that all these politicians have to worry about where ice-cream is being eaten, after all at least these kids are buying it!" "Someone has to help rebuild the Italian economy." Nick says.

Not wishing to remain on the subject of politics I steered the conversation back towards the town that we were sat in; Pieve San Stefano or *Città Del*

*Diario*, which translates to City of the Diary, it is a town well-known for collecting unpublished diaries, love letters and testaments written by everyday people, some which date back to the sixteenth century and are kept in the archives in the town hall. More than six thousand personal stories have been collected to date. Every year during the month of September a *Premio Pieve* literary prize is awarded. The winner's work is published and a monetary prize of one thousand euros is given to the lucky finalist.

There is a website where you can view excerpts of the works, some of them personal accounts of the horrors endured by local people during World War II. Many of the diaries are so moving that it is difficult not to shed a tear whilst reading them.

*

Another enjoyable day had seemed to pass so quickly. During the days we had taken to working long hours in the garden, but we had spent many of the evenings making new friends and socialising so we had formed firm friendships over the past months. This is what I love about the summers here, warm balmy evenings sat under the stars enjoying a drink or a light meal. By now it was mid-August, the 15th in fact and the beginning of the holiday period known to the Italians as *Ferragosto,* the word refers to the 'breaking of the seasons' the turning point, marking the end of the high temperatures of June, July and early August. Many Italians close their businesses and head for the coast, others to the hills to escape the last days of soaring temperatures; they too want to relax with family and friends during the last days of summer. Small hand written signs are hung in shop doors and windows advising of when the shop would be open again.

It was six o'clock the following evening when the shrill sound of my mobile phone announced that our friend Robin needed to speak to me, he was in the hospital at Citta Di Castello and they were keeping him in, at least for one night for observation. Yvonne being unable to drive had no idea how she was going to get home and we were only too happy to help. Robin had unknowingly driven all the way from England, at least one thousand miles with a detached retina. Treatment in Italy for such emergencies is swift and undertaken by some of the best surgeons in Europe and under reciprocal arrangements for European visitors, is usually free. Robin would be in safe hands and Yvonne would be in ours.

Nick and I had been invited to dine out on the terrace at the *Osteria Locanda Del Viandante* with a group of friends amongst the scarlet red geraniums and deep pink trailing petunias. We would be under the stars with magnificent views across the plains, south towards Umbria. From the terrace your eyes can follow the line of the Apennine hills as they disappear in the evening mists, the last of them only becoming indistinct near the city of Perugia, and the beautiful hillside town of Assisi, almost one hundred kilometres away. As the evening progresses the landscape turns from dark green to blue then finally black; as the twilight descends the lights of the towns sparkle and shimmer in the parallel lines of blue and white vapour that traverse the valleys and plains.

We left immediately, made sure that Robin was comfortable, collected Yvonne and arrived at the restaurant only fifteen minutes later than the table had been booked for. Near the small hamlet of Ponte alla Piera *Osteria Locanda Del Viandante* was once an ancient farmhouse nestling in the hillside that falls towards the deep gorge that harbours the river *Torrente Sovara*. On the opposite side of the valley you can sometimes just make out the distant shapes of deer grazing in a clearing as the cover of darkness and towering pine trees provide an element of safety for these shy nocturnal animals.

Every Friday evening throughout the month of August the restaurant hosts a live band and tonight the soft mellow tones of a young Italian singer called Nicola with an accompaniment of guitar, bass, keyboard and sometimes violin, provided a medley of songs from a selection as diverse as the Beatles and Amy Winehouse. Gentle and unobtrusive '*Pezzi Mancanti*' would delight our gathering well into the late hours.

For Nick and I, *antipasti* came in the form of deep fried courgette flowers or *fiori zucchini fritte* as they are called; the flowers are deep fried in a batter that just melts in the mouth. They are often stuffed with *ricotta* and spring onions and baked on the griddle. The secret when preparing the batter for the deep fried version is to use sparkling water in the recipe rather than still as it adds air to the mixture.

*

### *Deep fried Zucchini flowers*;

Fresh *Zucchini* flowers with the pistils removed
500ml Sparkling water
3 heaped tablespoons of plain flour
Pinch of salt

Lightly cover each *Zucchini* flower in the batter mixture and deep fry in Sunflower oil until light brown in colour.

Serve with quarters of a lemon and a dip of your choice.

*

Our visits to the *Osteria Locanda Del Viandante* became a regular occurrence throughout the summer as well as in the autumn and winter months that followed.

# CHAPTER 14

Yet another perfect day with a gentle warm breeze greeted me as the new day dawned beyond the unshuttered windows and a dry arid smell rose up from the garden. I wondered if the sunshine would ever end. It was shorts and polo shirts, white linen skirts, sleeveless tops and open sandals, the dress code never seemed to change; during the summer months the weather is always predictable.

We were to have lunch with our good friends David and Ernest at Citta Di Castello. On our last visit Nick needed to use the lavatory and was told to beware of the washing machine located in the corner, whenever in the spin cycle it gushed water all over the floor from a tear in the seal. David had bought a new seal with him from England intending to find a suitable engineer locally to carry out the work; a phase of the operation which is much more difficult than you would think. Nick and I had learnt that locating such a person was always easier said than done and determining the likely cost was stepping into completely unknown territory. An estimate was usually a figure plucked from the air and as soon as broken Italian with an English or American accent has been discovered, the higher the estimate goes. David and Ernest did not always have that much time to spare, so obtaining several estimates was not a real option especially when trying to tie someone down to within a specific window of opportunity. So the washing machine would have to continue leaking until their next visit. Nick was always up for a challenge and we tentatively agreed to have a go at replacing the door seal when they returned in a few weeks.

By eleven o'clock we were on our way heading south and looking forward to a convivial lunch with great company. We were armed with rough sketches and written instructions on how to replace the rubber door seal on an automatic washing machine and fresh memories of the 'You-Tube' video that we had watched over and over again. The man in the video said it would take no more than twelve minutes to replace the seal so we would have plenty of time before lunch, we hoped. We had all agreed thankfully, that it was worth the try and if it didn't work David and Ernest would have to get someone in.

It takes no more than forty minutes to get to Citta Di Castello, twenty of those minutes are spent on the notorious E45 dual-carriageway that never seems wide enough, even for a small car, let alone the huge juggernauts that thunder along its potholed surface on their way to Rome and Naples. Experience had taught Nick and I that you approach such vehicles in Italy rather like a cat stalking its prey. When you are fairly certain that the lorry driver has seen you in his wing mirror you hold your breath and make a dash for it. The passage between wheels that are taller than Rover and a crash barrier that has obviously witnessed too many miscalculated attempts is hair-raising to say the least.

We have seen lorries snaking their way up and down the E45 desperately trying to avoid the potholes, the drivers are totally oblivious to any other road user. As a major international highway that runs down the eastern side of Italy, it is frequently used by many of the old eastern block countries. The vehicles using the road, if that's what you would call them, often leave you speechless. So having stalked an array of lorries at a little over the hundred-kilometre speed limit we could see in the distance what I could only describe as a lopsided black blob. As we approached we could eventually recognise it as a car and that is a far as the similarity goes. Its suspension was so close to the ground that every time it went over a rise or sunk down in a pothole it sent up sparks that would compete with the very best fireworks you can buy. It swayed from side to side as the tyres tried to cope with the immense pressure bearing down on them, as it swayed, its cargo wobbled precariously from side to side. It was a small dark blue Volkswagen Polo on its roof, there was no rack, but there were two large mattresses, a sofa, a dining room table and chairs, legs pointing to the sky (some of the time) and half a dozen suit cases; the latter wrapped rather poorly in a clear plastic sheet which flapped violently in the wind. The mattresses reared up like wild horses with every gust. Closer inspection revealed that the whole load was secured in place by cargo straps that ran through open windows and clasped inside the car, presenting the passengers with every opportunity of garrotting themselves with every sway as they tried to avoid a mass of boxes, duvets and I dread to think what else. It looked as if the car was about to topple at any minute turning the dual carriageway into a car-boot sale. Nick pushed the accelerator pedal to the floor in a desperate attempt to pass. We had visions of the whole pile falling and the last thing we needed was to be hit by a flying mattress, try explaining that one to the insurance clerk when making a claim. The car was from Romania one of the newest members of the EU.

As we drove along the city walls of Citta Di Castello we noticed posters and banners depicting that unforgettable and iconic image of Marilyn Monroe by the American artist Andy Warhol who back in the sixties was a leading figure in the visual art movement known as Pop Art. There was an exhibition of his works being displayed in the renaissance *Palazzo Vitelli alla Cannoniera*, home of the Municipal Art Gallery. It was to run until the end of October and would comprise of seventy works, mainly from the Rosini Gutman and other private collections. I have been to a number of art exhibitions one of my favourites being the collection by the eccentric and surrealist painter Salvador Dali, which Nick and I had had the pleasure of seeing whilst visiting Rome. This particular exhibition I would however refrain from visiting, Warhol's style not to my particular taste, but I am sure of great interest to hundreds of other art lovers, after all his works included some of the most expensive paintings ever sold.

Fifteen minutes later we were standing in front of the aforesaid washing machine, wine glasses in hand discussing what had to be done and how.

Unfortunately, the sketch I had made happened to be for a different machine and not unsurprisingly the positioning of the screws were in a completely different place, which meant it was going to take a lot longer than we had originally envisaged. After some time had passed and after scrutinising the machine Nick and I agreed that it would be safer and probably easier to return on Monday, more suitably dressed, and armed with the relevant instructions and necessary tools. All in agreement and not needing any further encouragement the four of us downed tools and happily made our way to the restaurant and had a most enjoyable lunch.

We did return the following week as promised and this time we immediately set about the task in hand, the customary welcoming glass of red wine or chilled *Prosecco* which was served on arrival, was this time postponed until the job was complete, a steady hand and a clear head was required. I referred to our newly revised notes reading aloud the instructions step by step. Nick removed the springs, nuts, bolts and screws that were now visible, whilst I, having smaller hands and fingers tackled the more awkwardly placed. Nick and I worked well as a team and soon had the various facia panels and soap draw removed thus revealing a clear view of the workings together with the metal drum and seal. Nick then finally coerced the old grey plastic seal out and carefully manoeuvred and fitted the replacement, it was a fiddly job but fortunately Nick's conspiracy demon kept away and everything went according to plan. The man on the 'How to' Internet video had completed the whole task in the space of twelve minutes, although I think he cheated by unscrewing the relevant screws prior to starting the film. Nick and I funnily enough took a little longer, forty minutes to be exact; but thankfully achieved the same end result. After returning the machine to its original position it was the moment of truth. David turned the water back on and programmed the machine to run a short rinse cycle. The three of us peered anxiously through the window in the door as the metal drum began to fill with water. A towel was placed on the floor beneath, but not a dribble came from the door. They say 'needs must when the devil drives' and in Italy the devil often drives but there are always ways and means of getting things done. Nick and I had added yet another string to our bow!

*

Back at the Barn we settled down on the terrace to enjoy the last of the day's sunshine, the chirping of the cicadas overshadowed the melodious tones of the blackbird as it tried to compete for centre stage in the final hours before darkness. Our two petrol blue dragonflies or *libellula* as they are called in Italy chased each other around the pool like two fighter pilots locked in mortal combat. They were in the habit of flying just a little close to us for comfort at times, not that it really bothered us we were only too pleased that they came and shared our space. They

241

don't bite or sting and like our resident bat they spend a lot of their time feasting on mosquitoes and gnats.

The temperatures soared over the next few days and the pool remained the place to be. The refreshing yet now tepid water was a welcome relief to the hours spent enjoying the warmth of the sun, slowly and safely building up a nice tan. Nick would joke when in the company of friends that I had no white marks because I ran about the woods naked, yes there were times when I would take advantage of the privacy of our surroundings but always on the lounger with one eye watching out for that one unlikely Italian, determined to establish his legal 'right to roam,' but hey, I never ran around!

The following day yet another invitation to dinner arrived, this time from Anthony and Colin, Luca unfortunately was out of the country so we would not be able to enjoy his company on this occasion. As we turned off the main tarmac road we began descending the narrow hedge-lined track towards the valley below. This is a true white road, steep and well rutted by the summer thunderstorms and the subsequent rollercoaster humps and bumps left by two wheel drive vehicles desperately trying to find purchase in the loosened gravel. It also has a sharp turn but this has some advantage because as you change direction at the last bend you catch your first sight of the house, although not quite as dramatic as Joan Fontaine's first glimpse of Mandalay in Daphne Du Maurier's Rebecca the effect is similar, this is indeed a beautiful house and just as romantic.

'La Madera' dates back over four hundred years and was once a farmhouse, probably part of a *Borgo* or small hamlet, it has been beautifully restored. A lot of care and attention to detail has gone into retaining as much of the character and original features as possible. The interior is as spectacular as the exterior with a huge open plan chestnut beamed lounge and dining room, so tastefully decorated it could have come straight out of the pages of the Tuscan version of 'Homes and Gardens'. The rest of the house is equally sumptuous and created with an obvious flair for interior design. My eyes barely had time to rest upon any particular aspect of the house's charm, from the polished blood marble floor with the tiny red veins running through it, to the three white sofas positioned around the huge fireplace. This part of the room is an intimate and cosy place to relax. The opposite side of this large space is dedicated to dining, with views through the French style chestnut doors onto the stone terrace beyond. Open plan stairs take you down to another level where there is a large kitchen and separate apartment; once a huge *cantina* where the animals would have been kept, the heat from their bodies rising up through the ceiling to warm the rooms above. The view from every window across the twenty acres of farmland that drift down into the valley, is typically Tuscan with distant rolling hills and lines of cypress trees that make your eyes dart from one focal point to another. Next to the farmhouse there are various outbuildings, which are used for storage, one of which had already been converted into guest accommodation.

As we walked back into the lounge Colin was pouring the *Prosecco* and pangs of hunger produced by the delicate aromas rising from the kitchen were immediately banished upon the arrival of the appetisers. Small homemade triangular filo pastry parcels stuffed with goat's cheese, spinach and a hint of fennel. What can I say apart from they didn't last more than ten minutes; they were delightful.

The pre-dinner conversation turned to the chilling news, that within the small sleepy *comune* of Caprese Michelangelo rumours were afoot that members of the Mafia had visited certain people. It would not be wise to mention names but suffice to say that the presence of the local *Carabineri* increased tenfold as the Anti-Mafia squad were deployed. Two local people were subjected to, shall I say, criminal retribution after raising the alarm following some minor infringement of the planning laws. The vengeful reprisals that followed were fortunately carried out against property rather than people. Although there were apparently threats towards the latter, the perpetrators unleashed their anger against a tractor and for several months there beside a picturesque olive grove stood a hulk of charred metal and melted plastic, the remnants of apparently thirty thousand euros worth of machinery. The other whistle blower received a personal message scrawled in indelible paint across the internal walls of his newly built house, a message that might compel you to watch your back for the rest of your life.

Anthony is a great cook and served up *risotto* followed by stuffed pork, roasted potatoes and green beans, the meat so tender and perfectly cooked. To top it off we finished with an extremely indulgent homemade hot chocolate sponge pudding with ice-cream that was heavenly. Homemade *Limoncello* followed together with the usual *Grappa, Vin Santo* and coffee. The evening had been a pleasure to be part of as well as a gastronomic delight.

As we made our way up the lane to the Chestnut Barn Nick and I had our eyes fixed to the front ready to be the first to spot any one of our night-time visitors. It had become a regular game and the words "You're on pig alert" was the cue to begin. It was a clear balmy night, the stars bright overhead. As we rounded the last bend it was not a pig that confronted us, but caught in the beam of Rovers headlights was a *porcospino* (porcupine) it was very young and I was surprised to see it alone as usually they stay with their parents for the first few years of their lives. He or she broke into a gentle trot up the lane; we slowed our speed and cut the headlights to watch it in the light of the moon. Its black and white quills had fanned out and were raised high on its back in an attempt to make itself appear as if spoiling for a fight. Its little legs could clearly be seen beneath the display running as fast as they would carry it. We had often seen the family of three but nearly always at night, only once during the early hours of daylight. Slowly sensing that the threat had passed our youngster lowered its quills and disappeared amongst the undergrowth. A *porcospino* will, if it feels threatened, stamp its feet, whirr its quills and charge backwards towards an opponent with every intention of impaling it on its quills. The quills are then ejected to allow it to escape.

# CHAPTER 15

Seamus the Irish terrier came to stay for the two weeks that followed, Chris his owner had to return to England unexpectedly for family reasons. Seamus had been to the Barn several times and immediately made himself at home; his favourite spot during the day when we were both inside was next to Nick on the big blue sofa. At night he liked nothing more than to be snuggled up between us on the bed. Something I would not normally allow but if you could see the expression on his face and those big brown eyes you would see how easy it is to fall under his Irish charm.

Nick and I had often discussed having a dog of our own, we had even chosen a name and picked the breed, but as is always the case when working long hours and having other priorities, the thought was pushed to the back of our minds. Then there was the toing and froing from Italy, which also made it totally impracticable. Now after being here for some time we have come to the conclusion that it would not be fair on the dog. Our location nestled amongst the woods, as idyllic as it is, was one concern. There is no perimeter fence and with all the different scents and sounds, straying from the immediate vicinity would be far too much of a temptation for any dog to resist. Then there is the worrying reality that the dog may be poisoned or during the winter months taken by a hungry wolf which is not uncommon.

The poisoning of dogs that might pose a threat to the jealously guarded truffle grounds is also something that I find cruel beyond reason; but it happens all too often, those that do it will not discriminate between a trained truffle hunter and a domestic pet. Once, whilst out walking close to our Barn we came across a large piece of meat the size and quality not that dissimilar to the cut of beef you might serve up for Sunday lunch, to a family of six! When we went back the next day with a plastic bag with the intention of disposing of it, it had gone. Now we keep a refuse bag in Rover and a couple of bags in our walking coats just in case we come across something similar.

Hunting is a reality and even if like me, you hate the thought of a wild animal being killed it is something that you have to come to terms with living here. It is not unusual for a young child to bear witness to the slaughtering and butchering of an animal be it a wild boar, hare or rabbit. The legs of ham, *salame* and *salsicce* that hang above the open fireplaces curing are familiar sights to Italian children and no questions are asked. Here it is not an abhorrent act; it is a way of life, a tradition that is passed on through the generations. The animals that are bred have good lives, roaming free on the land, the hills and amongst the woods, eating natural foods, such as chestnuts, herbs and fruit, when it comes to slaughtering them, no part is wasted and full respect is shown. We have seen rabbits bred in the back yards of houses not as pets but for meat. Life in the mountains can be harsh, but it is the way of life in the country.

That evening, we drove to Fonaco a small hamlet
to the South of Monterchi which sits just on the
Tuscan Umbrian border, where our English friends
Roger and Susie and their impeccably behaved collie
dog, Renzo live. They divide their time between Italy
and England. We passed through fields filled with
sunflowers on the flat plains, their heads still
pointing in the direction of the sun but unfortunately
having now lost their sunshine golden glow to a
brown dry and drooping seed-head. We continued to
climb further up into the hills, passing fields of
walnut trees, which stood like regimented soldiers an
equal distance apart. Most are grown purely for their
wood, the nutritious and sweet fruit sadly ignored
and just left to rot, either that or there are some

serious producers of the drink *Nocino* living nearby. The wood is used predominately in the production of luxury furniture.

Just outside Fonaco we passed a deconsecrated church that had over several months benefited from extensive refurbishment, soon to be a home. It is sad to see beautiful little churches like this no longer being used as they were originally intended centuries ago. This building would once have been filled with *contadini,* the farm hands and their wives and children. Now the towering crane that hovers over a tall bell tower of natural stone with its arched windows and terracotta roof is evidence of an ever changing economic pattern, the countryside no longer able to support such communities; that way of life has passed. The new owners are probably wealthy Italian city workers who seek that idyllic country escape and who are we to say "How sad"? Without them the bell tower would have toppled and filled the adjacent land with rubble and scurrying lizards, now it is a beautifully landscaped garden. The builders have made a wonderful job of the restoration and when the crane has gone the scene will return to just as it was, all those centuries ago. The hills where the chestnut trees and oaks have been cleared are dotted with cypress trees and distinctive rows of vines with their leaning wooden supports sit intermingled with fields of silver olive and walnut groves. On the hill that separates Tuscany from Umbria sits the 12th century castle of Lippiano, its more than just impressive tower standing out proud against the skyline, this is Tuscany as we see it in postcards and calendars.

It was Roger's birthday and we had been invited to join him, Susie, Renzo and their close friends Richard Price, his wife Cathy and their daughter who were enjoying a short holiday. Richard is an antiquarian horologist who offers expert advice on the BBC television programme Antiques Road Show; we were amongst celebrities of the most modest and gentlemanly kind. At *La Pieve Vecchia* a restaurant on the outskirts of Monterchi we sat on the outdoor dining terrace under huge white parasols and watched the sun setting behind the fortified hilltop town, the cream coloured buildings turned to peach then orange and red as the sun bid its farewell for another day.

Renzo sat beneath the table and there was not a peep out of him, that was until he was surrounded by Italian children all wanting to give him a cuddle. We drank chilled *Prosecco* and toasted our generous host

Roger's good health with the wish of many more days just like these. The food courses arrived, with the usual platters of *antipasti, melone, crostini* and cold meat followed by either a *primi piatti*, which was normally a *pasta* or *risotto*, or *secondi piatti,* in the form of either a meat or fish dish. I opted to skip the *primi* and go straight for the duck with fruits of the forest sauce; it was without doubt a good choice. Nick chose the fillet steak cooked and covered with *tartufo nero* shavings, the aromatic perfume from the grated black *tartufo* is to us now unmistakable, and always leaves me feeling slightly heady.

\*

*Tartufi* come in all different shapes and sizes and can if used in a particular culinary dish increase the overall cost considerably, in some top restaurants the price charged is calculated per gram used. *Tartufi* can be found in a number of countries including France, Spain, Croatia, America as well as those in the southern hemisphere. They are a rare and valuable delicacy especially the Italian *tartufo bianco,* (white truffle). In 2010 the owner of a Chinese nightclub purchased two for the equivalent of £165,000.00, he also purchased one *tartufo bianco* that was found near Pisa in 2007 for a similar figure. There is nothing to compare with the flavour of *tartufo,* for me its more to do with its aroma, some compare it to that of chocolate which has been mixed with earth, a sort of musty, nutty fragrance, it just has to be tried! The black varieties are far less pungent than the more refined flavour and superior aroma of its creamy white counterpart. A *tartufo* is a knobbly type of fungus, which grows underground in between the soil and leaf litter around the roots of oak, chestnuts, birch and beech trees. The fungus relies on animals to eat it so that its spores can be dispersed. The *tartufo* draws water to the tree and in turn takes some of the nutrients. The fungus fruits from late summer through to early spring, depending on the variety. *Tartufai* (truffle hunters) generally gather them secretly. Dogs are often used to help locate the *tartufi*, as well as pigs; however pigs have a tendency to eat them immediately, as their scent is akin to that of the sex pheromone found in the saliva of a male pig. A dog is more interested in the reward it receives, than eating the truffle, a much safer option and a lot easier to transport to the hunting ground! Using small pieces of strong smelling cheese it can take up to four years to train a dog; after spending so much time and effort it is no wonder that the dog is worth its weight in gold so inevitably becomes vulnerable to poison attacks from rival *Tartufai*.

In Italy in 1985 it became illegal to use pigs for hunting as they were damaging the spores and causing the number of *tartufi* harvests to drop substantially. *Tartufi*, especially the highly sought after white variety, are highly valued by chefs and restaurateurs the world over, and are usually very expensive outside of their host countries. In parts of Northern Italy and Umbria where *tartufi* are the key ingredient used in many local dishes the price is much less prohibitive. The *tartufi bianchi* unlike the *tartufi neri* that are eaten raw or lightly cooked, are far too delicate to be cooked and are used only in their raw form. Simple dishes of freshly made *tagliatelle* are transformed by sprinkling a small amount of grated *tartufo bianco* over the top; it is also a great addition to scrambled eggs. *Tartufi* can also be used to flavour ice cream or *gelato*. '*Tre Scalini*', 'Three steps' a restaurant famous for this signature dish overlooks the *Piazza Navona* in Rome.

*Tartufi* are also the star attraction at the Citta Di Castello *Tartufo Bianco Festa*, which is held annually from the end of October until the beginning of November. This year the 34th festival will take place in the beautiful setting of the *Piazza Matteotti, in* the centre of the town, overlooked by none other than the six elegant former palaces or *palazzi*. Here you can sample and buy affordable portions of *tartufo* as well as products infused with the flavour, such as oils, cheeses, *salame* and sauces. This is a must visit festival for all food lovers; there is always a lot to see and do such as cooking demonstrations by top Italian chefs, and talks from the *Tartufai*.

It is possible to buy *tartufi* from various places, small *tartufi nero* can be found for sale in tiny glass jars at the local supermarket or delicatessen style shops all year round, however to buy fresh you need to keep an eye open at the local markets. There are two towns near the Barn one called Le Ville and the other Pieve San Stefano where you can often see a makeshift white board by the side of the road with the words *tartufi vendesi* or *porcini* depending on what is available that day. When it comes to storing *tartufi* there are many conflicting opinions the one consensus being that they are best used fresh. *Tartufi* release their aroma continually until it is totally exhausted, the rate accelerating on exposure to air. Either the strong pervasive fragrance disappears into the air or it pervades any other absorbent item kept in its close proximity. At the same time the *tartufi* will also dehydrate. After thorough cleaning to remove any remaining soil, they need to be kept in their own sealed containers. The best way to preserve their aroma is to emulate their natural underground habitat. The preferred item in which to do this is uncooked rice. *Tartufi* need their moisture to preserve their aroma and should not be allowed to dry out. The rice protects the natural moisture within them, whilst preventing them getting damp from excess moisture that could lead them to decay. Once suitably covered they can be stored in a cool, dark place ideally a refrigerator where they can be kept for up to three weeks. As they are used, the scented rice can be cooked as a separate dish. Any variety of rice is suitable for preserving *tartufi*, however *Arborio* rice found in Italy, if used can later be made into a delicious *tartufo* infused risotto.

*

That night we went to bed quite exhausted after being in wonderful company and immensely enjoying the food and drink. With so many people of all nationalities having second homes here, this time of year is one round of socialising after another and as wonderful as it is there are times when a night in comes as a welcome change. In the early hours of the morning I was woken by a tremendous thunderclap and the sound of heavy rain and hailstones bouncing off the roof. Hail is quite common here in the mountains even in summer. One year the hailstones were so large Rover was peppered with small dents caused by the force of the storm.

With our windows open wide to allow the cool night air to fill the bedroom, the insect nets were all that separated us from the elements. I began to estimate the distance of the storm counting the seconds between the flashes of lightning and the thunderclap that followed, just like a child, 'one elephant, two elephant, three elephant' it was getting closer every second. I had visions of the enormous pine trees that stood only metres from the Barn crashing through the thick stonewalls that protected us. A sound like an express train speeding past just feet away was the wind that rolled up the valley, no longer in gusts but a continuous roar following after the storm as it made its way north. I could see the tops of the firs below the Barn in the lightening, bending almost double before springing back, I was amused to find myself thinking of heavy rock band groupies 'head banging' on an unseen dance floor. In the next breath they would fling themselves in the other direction dark dancing silhouettes against the backdrop of the mountain behind.

The rain and the hail were unceasing as my thoughts turned to a little dog, called Poldino. He belongs to Tina; a lady who we had stayed with on a few occasions whilst sorting out our Barn and had fondly nicknamed *Nonna*, the Italian word for grandmother. Poldino, like most dogs in this area is kept outside. England is a nation of dog lovers where our pets share the same space; it came, as something of a shock to find that Italians don't have the same affinity with their animals. Night and day he is to be found attached to a five-metre length of chain fastened to a wooden barrel where an entrance has been rustically shaped into its lid. When turned on its side it made the perfect kennel. Although clearly much loved he is fed on scraps of food left over from the table and given two short walks each day; on nights like these I imagined him cowering in the corner of his barrel and shaking.

Dogs in Tuscany are mainly kept for hunting, for protection or to deter wild boar from entering gardens and causing devastation with their snouts in search of food. In the Northern towns such as Turin and Milan you do come across dogs that are best described as 'accessories', their heads often found peeking out from the pockets of designer handbags.

Most are working dogs like the *Maremma* that specifically look after the sheep *pecore* and other livestock. You can often see a flock of *pecore* wandering the hills and in amongst them would be two or more *Maremma*, similar in size and stature to a Pyrenean mountain dog although white or pale cream in colour, they are there to guard and protect their flock against the *lupo* that roam the Tuscan countryside after dusk. I once watched a herd of sheep being rounded up by two of these incredible animals into the corner of a field beneath overhanging trees, there was storm passing much like the one I have described and they instinctively moved their wards to a place of relative safety and shelter.

My storm continued for a large part of the night and early morning, both Nick and I were left feeling almost as tired as when we went to bed the night before, it did not however dampen our spirits as today was a day that Nick and I had been looking forward to for the past couple of weeks. Helen had arranged for us, Mick and our two Danish friends, Borge and Jytte to be part of a wine tasting tour at a Vineyard known as 'Villa La Ripa', on the outskirts of the nearby town of Arezzo, at Antria.

Borge and Jytte live in California, having emigrated some years ago from their homeland of Denmark. They spent some of the summer here in their beautiful house, which nestles into the side of the hill on the historic mound of Caprese Michelangelo where the great artist himself was born; the views from their house are extraordinary.

It was a beautiful day; our tour was booked for eleven o'clock. A straight, tree-lined white road several hundred metres long can be seen through the impressive entrance gates and high walled enclosure. Immaculately kept, the gentle incline sweeps away from you up towards the Villa. As the electronically controlled gates swing open an obviously important building partly obscured by mature cypress trees can be seen in the distance. A tower standing proud above the roof is the first hint of its Renaissance pedigree. Thousands of vines and row after row of olive trees line the gentle slopes and abut the drive; not a scrap of land is wasted.

The magnificent Villa suddenly appears as you walk up the last fifty metres of lawned steps and a grand gravel frontage opens out before you, here the property owner Saverio Luzzi greeted us. We started the tour with a visit to the formal garden, which sits to the right of the Villa it is enclosed and gated. As you enter you cannot fail to take in the wonderful scent of jasmine clinging to the ancient walled garden and the recessed alcoves containing statues. In the centre stands a replica of the instantly recognisable 'Faun' discovered in the ancient city of Pompeii in the South of Italy; even here the mosaic floor on which it stands is also in keeping with that of the original. The beautifully kept garden offers a cool and tranquil space in which to relax and take in the views out across Arezzo and to the hills that lay beyond.

Next we visited the cave or cellar where the huge wooden barrels filled with maturing wine are kept. Some of the casks made from American oak are only used four times before being replaced, a costly but necessary exercise in order to achieve and maintain the quality of the wine produced at this vineyard. In the same cave the process of making a fine wine is explained the purpose of metal vats where the grapes ferment, the gases that are added at various stages is all introduced to our group of enthusiastic wine drinkers.

The Vineyard is relatively small in terms of production; the area of land, only two hectares in size produces seven thousand bottles of wine per year, which is just over one bottle per vine. Saverio is happy with this number and does not wish to expand production or export his wines abroad, he wants to sell to local restaurateurs and to those he has had the pleasure of meeting on his wine tasting tours. Wine is Saverio's passion but not his profession; he is in fact a psychiatrist in Arezzo. His wine is of incredible quality and deserves to be at the top of its class. His obvious enthusiasm comes over in his address to the gathering as does his charm and friendliness. He loves to share his knowledge and the fascinating story of how he came to buy the Villa and how the wine venture came about.

Initially Saverio had no intention of producing wine; the vines had been neglected over several years when the house had remained unoccupied after the last owner had died. In his profession he met an experienced wine producer, whilst in discussion with him he related that he intended to remove the old vines and landscape the garden. The wine producer was shocked at this seemingly casual remark about destroying the vines that had grown there for several hundred years. So much so he offered to tend them and teach Saverio how to look after the vines, free of charge for a year. The venture was a success and the wines produced now are worthy of high praise.

On entering the Villa we were led into a small room with all its original features and although it was last decorated in 1780 they seemed as fresh as if they had been finished yesterday. The walls and ceiling are covered in a fresco detailing a climbing plant like ivy, which gives the impression that you are seated beneath a pergola. Beautifully painted birds hidden amongst the foliage bring to mind the picture of a garden in summertime. The central table and armchairs, all original Renaissance pieces, are elegant and stylish.

It was in this room that we had the opportunity to taste the Villa La Ripa's only Rose wine called *Spaziolibero*, which is made using 50 percent of the Sangiovese grape and 50 percent Syrah. This wine is apparently the most difficult to produce and during thirteen years of trying only two harvests have been successful, it has a clean, dry and refreshing taste, which makes it a good *aperitivo* or accompaniment to starters, fish or light dishes.

Villa La Ripa has thirty-five rooms, which are home to Saverio Luzzi and his wife Adriana. One of the original owners of the house was from the Gualtieri Family and a friend of the Medici's, a powerful and well-documented Tuscan family. The Villa certainly has its share of history, in the 19th century after Napoleons troops invaded the nearby town of Arezzo the Villa was confiscated and put up for sale by auction and it passed to the noble Ubertini family; one of their member led the Aretine forces in a famous battle against the Florentines.

Before the main wine tasting the small group of wine enthusiasts followed our host to a delightful little private Chapel; in this small family chapel behind the ornately dressed altar there is a 16th century painting of an angel blessing the Villa and its grounds. The large, almost heftily proportioned angel stands on high, her left hand sweeping over the pastoral scene of the estate and house; the same house, the same gravel drive and the same vines rolling down the slight incline towards the entrance gates. Little, if anything has changed on the estate since the artist applied the paint all those years ago. Internally modern plumbing and heating are the only 21st century additions that the new owners have discretely added for their own comfort.

Now we would start the wine tasting and we are led away to a long dining hall with vaulted ceilings of herringboned terracotta tiles. In the centre of the room is a long dining table with benches on either side. At the end of the room a high curved arch seems to beckon you through into a comfortable lounge where a huge white stone fireplace takes centre stage, in this room there are comfortable regency style chairs in richly textured green silks set within gold ormolu style, ornate frames. In the centre of this there is a small table draped in white lace, a white roman style porcelain urn with a raised floral pattern sits on the lace, within the urn are half a dozen large bright yellow sunflowers surrounded by what looks very like strands of barley but must surely be Tuscan grasses. Someone has a good eye for décor! For the tasting however we would be sitting on the benches in the dining hall.

The first of the wines arrived carefully carried by Saverio's charming assistant who knows just how to measure each pour ensuring so that each person around the table receives an equal measure from the bottle. Saverio describes the flavours that we should be able to detect, deep ruby red fruity with cherries and hints of cinnamon are words that describe the wine that is produced using 100% Sangiovese grapes. The texture is smooth, harmonious and persistent with strong tannins, ideal with every kind of *pasta* and meat. He speaks perfect English and has a natural relaxed delivery that exudes passion for his subject; you feel as though you have known him for years. During this relaxed atmosphere questions were raised about the wine, about the Villa, the olives, the land and the soil, so important for the grape.

He recalled the memory of a discovery that was made between 1996 and 1997; Before moving into the Villa, he had enlisted the help of some trades people to see if there were any original features or frescoes hidden behind the stark white interior walls of the chapel, after some months, sadly he was advised there was nothing to reveal. One day after lunch, Saverio retired to bed for his daily siesta to escape the summer heat and relax after a typical long and filling Tuscan lunch. His wife however had not been convinced that the builders were right. She drove to the Villa, taking with her a bucket of water and some cloths. She began carefully washing a small patch of the wall inside the Chapel and was amazed when she came across blue paint hidden beneath the clinical white surface, she continued washing the wall carefully, and a fresco appeared; immediately she rang Saverio. Saverio still half asleep had not even realised that she had left the house. More ancient frescoes were later uncovered within the first floor rooms.

*Peconio* was the name of the first of the red wines and having explored the merits Saverio told us of how the wine came to be named. In the garden while digging he discovered buried deep within the soil close to the Villa a piece of carved marble, it was not renaissance in style but Roman, it looked like part of a top section of a Roman column. Curious to know more about the origins of the Villa, Saverio found an old book written by an archaeologist who whilst digging in the grounds of the Villa over two hundred years ago found the remains of an old Roman bath or *thermae*, and part of the Roman Villa that had stood on same spot some 2000 years earlier. The wine was named after the owner of the Villa at that time.

The next wine we sampled was called *Tiratari*; his daughter Claudia named this one. When she was a child she had been reading a story about a dreamland where everything was beautiful and good, the land was called *Tiratari*. When Claudia first visited the Villa after her parents had completed the purchase she said 'here we are at *Tiratari*' so the wine had been appropriately named. The grape blend is a mixture of 85% Sangiovese, and 15% Merlot and Shiraz.

Claudia is now a pharmacist who by way of a sideline makes cosmetics from the grapes and olives produced on the Estate. Unfortunately we did not get to meet her, but we did get to sample some of her products of hand cream and moisturisers. The Estate also produces an olive oil that can be bought and once again Saverio has excelled, winning a Silver Medal at the 'New York International Olive Oil Competition', something that he is obviously very proud of.

The *Tiratari* wine was an even bigger success with the eleven of us sat around the table. Glasses were held up to the light, swirled around and sniffed, behaving like the professionals we were not. We were experiencing an aroma of spiced aromatic wood and red fruits; it is elegant and smooth on the tongue, the deep ruby red liquid clings to the glass leaving trails and lines; we were told that this is a sign of a good wine. Cheese was passed around the table together with some crackers and we chatted amongst ourselves while the final and most treasured wine was brought to the table.

*Psyco,* Saverio's top wine named as such for obvious reasons but its title seems to belittle the beautiful liquid that rests within. Another bright ruby red coloured wine, which has spent 12 months in French oak barrels before being bottled and stored for another 12 months. The aroma is intense, again with hints of red fruits, we are starting to appreciate that the taste is indeed elegant, smooth, harmonious but with strong tannins and although they are all especially good tasting wines this is indeed a superior wine. The grapes used are 50% Sangiovese and 50% Cabernet Sauvignon. All that remained now was to decide which wine and how many bottles to buy...

It was a day that we would remember; the sheer scale and beauty of the property overwhelming, our visit made all the more memorable by the fabulous exclusive wines and the company of our perfect host Saverio Luzzi.

# CHAPTER 16

Today we made a trip to Gubbio, a place that we had planned to visit for a number of months but had never done so. The town lies to the south east of the Barn and every year competes in the crossbow competition with our nearest major town of Sansepolcro. The bowmen of Sansepolcro travel to Gubbio in May each year to compete in the competition in honour of Saint Egidio. The bowmen of Gubbio make the return visit to Sansepolcro on the second Sunday in September during the 'Balestra' when many of the townsfolk dress in medieval clothing for the festival.

The SS19 exits the E45 and then snakes its way through a deep gorge where tall poplar trees line the valley. Open fields, south facing vineyards and olive groves create patchworks that bring relief to the density of the wooded areas that fill the hills above. The road is popular with the huge transport Lorries, a link to the west from the busy port of Ancona, East on the Adriatic coast to the E45 and A1 roads; so this road is often frequented by 'working girls' of all different nationalities, shapes and sizes. It is similar to the final approach of the dual carriageway that runs into Arezzo from Anghiari. Here they sit on plastic patio chairs or simply stand in lay-bys waiting for their next client, often scantily clothed they brave the elements for most of the daylight hours. One of the more mature ladies can often be seen dangling a bare leg from inside the driver's seat of her camper van. They stand; alone their vulnerability is terrifying. This is not the picture that normally springs to mind when you think of *Bella Italia* but it's a reality all the same.

*

We drove through the suburban areas of Gubbio or *frazione* as they are called and finally began to follow the signs to the *centro* past the remains of the Roman amphitheatre that was built at the end of the first century. Renovation works have been carried out and the ruin now plays host to a number of classic productions that are put on during the balmy summer evenings. The town is much bigger than we had envisaged and after finding the tourist information office we sat in the *Piazza dei Quaranta Martiri*, the square named after the forty martyrs who were tragically executed on the 22<sup>nd</sup> June 1944. Forty Italians were chosen at random, victims of a reprisal execution for the loss of the life of one Nazi soldier shot by partisans. There is a Mausoleum on the outskirts of the centre of the town on *Via Perugia* where their remains lie in the individual tombs that line the walls. There are thirty-eight men entombed here the youngest was 17 years old. A 61-year-old mother and her 31-year daughter also lie amongst them. A few feet away is the preserved section of the wall where they were executed by firing squad, the wall bears the scars to this day, it is a sad sight...

Gubbio is full of impressive buildings the *Palazzo dei Consoli* which was built between 1332 -1338, being one of the most beautiful public halls in all of Italy. To the left of the building is the crenellated bell tower where the big bell or *Il Campanone,* which weighs two tonnes and dates back to 1769, can be found. The bell ringers apparently ring the bell using their feet. The main building now houses the Municipal Museum where there are various collections displayed from the 6$^{th}$ century BC right up to the 19$^{th}$ century. The Museums most treasured possession being the world famous Eugubine Tablets, seven bronze tablets engraved with religious rites, the most

extensive text of the ancient western world, ever to have been discovered and the most important text in the Umbrian language.

The town is a mix of medieval, Gothic and Renaissance architecture; the houses and palaces tower above you climb ever higher through narrow streets to another level on the lower slopes of Mount

Ingino. The grey limestone buildings almost take on a yellow hue in the bright sunlight. Tourist shops selling postcards, model crossbows and religious memorabilia together with pots and plates in every colour and style imaginable, are everywhere you look.

The *Colle Eletto* cable car was so named after Dante's reference to the mountain in his Divine Comedy, Canto XI of the Paradiso, his words '*Intra Tupino e l'aqua che discende dell colle eletto del beato Ubaldo, fertile costa d'alto monte pende*', which loosely translated mean 'Between Tupino and the water that descends the chosen hill of blessed Ubaldo, a fertile slope of the lofty mountain hangs.' The cable car began running in December 1960 and resembles a cage just big enough to take two people. The locals refer to the cages as *buzzi*, a word meaning waste bins in the local dialect. The car connects the town to the convent and Basilica of Saint Ubaldo, a former Bishop of Gubbio. The saint died in 1160 and his remains are now kept within a Neo Gothic Urn, which sits above the high altar. The cable car runs from near the *Porta Romana* gate, although the convent and Basilica can also be reached by car if you have no head for heights!

With our stamina beginning to wane after walking up and down the steep narrow streets, through low vaulted alleyways and beautiful lush green gardens, we decided to find a suitable place for lunch. Menus are purposefully placed for maximum exposure outside every restaurant and bar along your route, but we made a beeline for the *Ristorante La*

*Balestra*, which has a beautiful outside dining terrace to the rear overlooking the bell tower of the church of San Giovanni.

A waitress showed us to our table for two in the sunlight next to an older Italian couple. After ordering a light lunch and choosing a suitably priced bottle of red wine, one of Nick's old favourites by the Antonelli vineyard, *Montefalco Rosso* 2009, we settled down to admire the views from the terrace and began reading about places of interest that there are to visit. Within minutes our food arrived which was enough to feed five people rather than just the two of us. The Italian couple were smiling nodding and raising their glasses in our direction, keen perhaps to make new acquaintances. The lady rose from her chair for the photo that her partner was encouraging her to pose for seated on the stonewall terrace with the glorious view behind her. Quick as a flash just as the camera shutter clicked my ever-mischievous husband jumped onto the wall beside her and put his arm around her. Who was this strange man? I could see our Italian neighbour asking himself. The lady laughed and eventually so did her husband, who was a very well built and obviously capable of looking after himself, in fact he looked just like a mafia don from Naples.

At that moment I remembered the wise words of our real estate agent when I told him we were driving down to Naples for a few days.'

"Catherine", he said with the usual shrug of the shoulders a resigned gesture "you go to Naples in your car; you come back on the train".

Feeling a little embarrassed and slightly uneasy I smiled and offered words of apology telling her that my husband could become a little playful after a couple of glasses of red wine. She replied that her husband was just the same and at that very moment he gulped back the remaining wine in his glass, raised the empty bottle to the sky and began shaking it frantically whilst laughing out loud. The next thing I knew I was taken by the hand and seated next to his wife on the wall, and after sharing a *digestivo* with them we were best of friends, that's how it is in Italy, there's never a dull moment.

Back on the streets we made our way towards the church of *San Francesco della Pace,* a church I had wanted to visit as it was built during the first half of the 17th century on the site of the cave where legend states that the wolf that had tormented the Gubbio townsfolk lived. It also houses the stone that is said to have born witness to the pact between St Francis and the wolf. Unfortunately the church was closed when we arrived so I will have to return another day. The church also homes the medium sized *Ceri*, a tall heavy wooden structure on which a statue is placed and then carried through the streets on the shoulders of the *Ceri* bearers. The festival or race takes place on the eve of the feast of the patron Saint Ubaldo on 15th May every year. Gubbio hosts many such events throughout the year. At Christmas time the outline of a massive Christmas tree is set out on the slopes of Monte Ingino. Twenty kilometres of cable is used to power the eight hundred lights. It can be seen from the 7th December until January 10th.

We made our way up towards the Ducal Palace, past the Diocesan Museum with its gigantic old 'Canons' Barrel' that can hold nineteen thousand, three hundred and fifty litres of wine. The barrel can be seen through the bars of a large window; its impressive size and structure towers above you. You wonder how the Coopers could have made a container on this scale that would hold wine without a single leak.

Next we strolled through the imposing entrance gate to the *palazzo* where a beautifully formed vaulted ceiling cast a welcome shadow over the herringbone patterned stone floors. This is probably the highest point of the town and what is in effect a portico leads you out onto a square containing formal gardens. Low box bushes form paths that in turn lead you towards a viewpoint from where you can take in the whole town and surrounding countryside. The panoramic views from here are astonishing; as you look down on the tower of the *Palazzo dei Consoli* the jumbled roofs spread out below you and the warmth of the afternoon sun radiates from the different shades of terracotta tile.

# CHAPTER 17

Miss September was leant over the bonnet of a sports car; between her naked breasts she held a red hosepipe and squirted water up beneath her chin. Water dripped from her elbow and other prominent parts of her body. A tiny pair of unbuttoned Denim shorts covered what little remained of her modesty. The *Pirelli* calendar was placed high on the wall for all to see. This was a place rarely visited by women. The concrete floor beneath the workbench was strewn with mechanical engine parts of all shapes and sizes. Tools hung from boarded walls, their shapes carefully drawn to make sure the correct tool was returned to its resting place. A well used strimmer; a very sad looking lawnmower and a number of chainsaws gave away the secrets of this location where the smell of engine oil hung in the air. On one side of the room three elderly men sat on an ancient bench, not waiting for anything just there for the company and the conversation. They turned towards the two strangers who had just entered, the ding of the bell above the door giving us away, the look of surprise at the sight of a woman in their presence brought the conversation to a sudden halt; no Italian lady would have entered such a den of iniquity. The man in brown overalls nodded in acknowledgement of our arrival, but the chain he was sharpening on the rotating wheel continued its journey through the machine, the grinding metal threw sparks of light into the shadows at the corner of the room. The chain was removed and the process began again until both sides of the teeth on the loop were shining and dangerous once more. We were here to collect Nick's chainsaw but we had to wait until another two chains had passed through the grinder and the man in the brown overall could give us his undivided attention.

The nights were drawing in, the days shortening and the evenings had lost some of the humidity that followed the rainstorms of August. The evening air was fresh and soon the fires would have to be lit once again, autumn was closing in and within just a few weeks the first hint of rusty hues would appear in the forest around the Barn. The chestnut harvest would begin all around us and the festivals in the villages would attract local people, there to meet in numbers perhaps for the last time until the arrival of spring.

We were nearing the end of the first year of our new Italian life and it had not all been plain sailing. I would often wonder at his thoughts and would cringe when something hadn't gone to plan, but the moment would pass and I was pleased that for both of us the good times seemed to outweigh the frustrations. There were times when I too thought that Italian bureaucracy would get the better of me and I knew that on more than one occasion Nick was in favour of 'throwing in the towel'.

During the next few months we would be preparing for winter, hours of wood sawing and chopping would be needed in order to fuel the wood burners to heat the Chestnut Barn. The chainsaw was now in the best of health and after buying two spare chains we took our leave from the den of iniquity and decided to combine our visit with a trip to the nearby hilltop town of Citerna just a few miles south of Le Ville where the chainsaw had spent the last few weeks.

Citerna, a town which lies thirty kilometres south east of the Chestnut Barn, sits on the border of Tuscany and Umbria and is classed as one of Italy's most beautiful medieval hilltop villages, having featured in the *'Borghi più Belli d'Italia'* (most beautiful villages in Italy) competition. The city walls which protect the heart of Citerna were built between the $13^{th}$ and $14^{th}$ century and are entered by two gates one to the north, *Porta Fiorentina* and to the south *Porta Romana*, both named after the towns in which direction they face, Florence and Rome.

I would describe this fortified hill town as small and beautiful, the views from the top alone are worth the visit, and there is also much to be discovered when it comes to its history and works of art. In the church of *San Francesco* you can view an exquisite terracotta statue of the 'Madonna and Child', that was discovered in 2001 by the art historian, Laura Ciferri, who was studying renaissance terracotta works in Umbria. After four years of scrutiny by various experts in Florence, the Madonna and Child was finally attributed to Donatello, the famous Florentine renaissance artist. After much painstaking work it has been restored to its original state. The statue dates between 1415 and 1420 and stands at one hundred and fourteen centimetres tall. The faces of both the Madonna and Child are truly captivating, the sculptured creases of the Madonna's flowing gown give the impression of carved marble but the whole form is made in terracotta. The Citerna tourist information office offers a guided tour of the church and a visit to the temperature controlled side room where she is housed under lock and key. The village, once a fortress takes its name from the word *cisterna* meaning cistern, and today the extensive network of channels, tanks and vaults that lie below the village have been fully excavated and restored and can also be seen on this tour, for the princely sum of five euros.

Another unique feature of the village is the medieval arched walkway or *camminamento medievale* which circles most of the east and west sides of the town. It passes through the base of the fortified walls, part of which is known as *Via degli Innamorati*, or 'road of the lovers'. The far-reaching panoramas from both 'the road' and the main *Piazza Scipioni*, stretch across the flat plains to *La Verna* in the north and the peaks of Monte Sibillini in the South. It was here in the summer of 1849, that Guiseppe Garibaldi the Italian General and politician, together with some of his troops took respite and stayed overnight, whilst being hunted by the Austrians, Spanish, French and Neapolitans, on their way to Ravenna. This led to Citerna becoming one of the first Umbrian towns to be part of the new Kingdom of Italy in 1861 following the *risorgimento* or unification of Italy, which took place on March 17<sup>th</sup> 1861.

*

With mid morning fast approaching we left Citerna behind us and made our way back towards Anghiari passing through the flat plains which at this time of year are covered in Kentucky tobacco plants, the tractors and trailers were scattered amongst the rows of massive plants. Dark skinned migrant workers stoop to pick the huge green leaves tying the stalks makes small bundles, and with stalks pointing to the sky they are placed on the wooden drying racks before being lifted on the trailers and taken to the drying houses.

Tobacco is big business here in the Valtiberina but its presence brings with it mixed emotions. The local people are understandably concerned at the health risks associated with smoke coming from the many drying houses situated throughout the valley. The controversy will undoubtedly continue especially as the local producers were given the go ahead for thirteen new projects, much of them funded using European Union money. Newly constructed dryers and barns have now popped up on the plains near Motina and San Leo, in close proximity to houses; the smoke from the drying process can be seen drifting in the air. The Kentucky tobacco is the variety used in the making of Tuscan cigars. In Sansepolcro an ice-cream bar has introduced a tobacco-flavoured ice cream. Other retailers have produced tobacco-flavoured *salame*, mature cheeses as well as chocolate.

Anghiari is a town famous for its links with medieval history and there are many artisan activities going on in unseen backstreet workshops. Furniture restoration is one example, not immediately apparent to the passer-by. Anghiari has become a centre of excellence and is home to the *Istituto Statale d'Arte*. This is a secondary school that offers a five-year course studying the art of furniture making, restoration, inlay, carving and gilding, together with the restoration of paintings, religious icons and relics.

*Busatti* the famous and world-renowned lace and linen makers are also present in the town, their premises are located in Via Mazzini. The *Busatti* family has run the business for 170 years and they take great pride in their fabrics. You can visit the factory and workshop, which is situated below the shop, and see the linens being made. The raw thread is treated with olive oil before being spun and woven, it is then dyed using only *Busatti* colours, a derivative of natural produce, such carrots, onions, sage, and henna.

The town was bustling with Italians, as Wednesday is market day, a market has been held here since the 13th century. All of the shops in the narrow flag-stoned streets were open and we slowly made our way down the steep streets to the main *piazza*. Several stalls offer a vast array of produce including clothing, linen and bedding, leather goods, shoes, socks and undergarments. A large selection of foods, all at very reasonable prices are also available. Part of the market is held in *Piazza IV Novembre* situated beyond the *Galleria di Magi* a large arch just off the main thoroughfare of *Giacomo Matteotti*. The arch built in 1889, is named after the Venetian engineer, Girolamo Magi who built it.

Looking down on the *Piazza IV Novembre* is the beautiful theatre known now as *Teatro Comunale*, which was built in 1789. Ten marble statues surmount the theatres façade. Inside there are three floors housing thirty-eight boxes, all beneath a beautifully frescoed ceiling. The building was restored in 1985 and today is still home to many shows as well as conferences.

We found a table at the bar that sits at the foot of the theatre where we enjoyed a coffee whilst watching the world go by. Access to this part of Anghiari was restricted to vehicles both moving and parked, metal barriers prohibiting their access. Here there were three big clothes stalls and a fruit and vegetable stall. There was also a plant stall, a linen stall, a sweet stall, similar to the old pic and mix style sweets sold in Woolworths back in the 80's and two food stands. One was selling a variety of Tuscan *salame*, cheeses, wines and oils, the other *Porchetta,* which is roasted pork, boned, rolled and stuffed with various herbs and garlic. It is popular all over Italy but is said to have originated from a province in Rome. They also sold cooked chickens, the two lines of roasting poultry rotating continuously on a spit. A queue of older Italian women formed, buying not only whole chickens but also roasted diced potatoes flavoured with aromatic *rosmarino*. We watched the men watching the women, the men made no attempt to disguise their interest as heads rotated as if watching a tennis match in slow motion.

The church bells in all corners of the town sounded the one o'clock chime, not one synchronised bell amongst them, it was like they were calling to each other like town elders "that's it, tell them to stop". The stallholders slowly began the laborious task of packing away their unsold goods and reloading them into their scruffy white vans.

On Sunday mornings what is perhaps ambitiously called an antiques market is held in *Piazza Baldaccio*, 'bric a brac' is a better term, on occasion you can find interesting tools used by the artisans of years gone by; rustic in appearance they make good ornaments to hang in the *loggia*. The quality of many of the items on display is, sadly poor; most of it is unjustifiably expensive and bartering often proves fruitless.

# CHAPTER 18

Before the winter finally set in we would have to touch base with England and make the long drive back across the continent. As an English car, insured by a British company, Rover would have the usual tests to be legal and safe for another year. A costly affair yet again I'm afraid and the repairs meant that we had to extend our stay, whilst waiting for parts to arrive.

My Birthday that falls towards the end of October had been a disappointment, the time spent in and out of Land Rover dealerships and the MOT bay would not easily be forgotten. But now we were almost ready to leave, a final visit to a rented shipping container that held many of our stored personal items to fill Rover to the gunnels and we would be off back to Italy.

Ever changing colours marked the journey, a wet summer in England gave rise to a golden autumn; but as the miles sped by towards Lyon in France and then on to Italy, the land seemed to cling to the last vestiges of summer. The Aosta valley, the Alpine pass that is staggeringly beautiful at anytime of the year was turning, the vines high on the foothills almost a deep red now would all too soon be covered in the first dustings of snow.

We had been away far longer than we expected and for the next few weeks it would be 'all hands to the pumps', to ready ourselves for our own winter. Wood for the fires would have to be cut and there were several chestnut trees that had died during the summer as a result of a virulent strain of parasite, these needed clearing out. The wood, already seasoned and bleached by the sun would burn nicely in the wood-burners; but the trees had to be felled and chopped into logs to fit neatly into them. There was always the added danger when working in the forest from the end of September through to February, that of the hunters. The hunters have an automatic right to hunt on anyone's land. So within a few days Nick and I would be dressed in the most visible old clothes we could find, with bright orange hardhats and red ear defenders and making as much noise as possible as we approached the first fated chestnut tree. The chainsaw once up and running would scare any wild boar far away from the Barn and in turn the hunters in pursuit would know that they would be wasting their time coming near. A stray bullet was always a concern, especially at weekends when all and sundry were out, hoping to bag themselves a *cinghiale* to butcher and freeze for Christmas!

Today however was Sunday, in fact Remembrance Sunday so the trees could wait we would be remembering those British and Italian men and women who gave their lives in the service of their country. Situated on the Tuscan/Umbrian border is the nearby hilltop town of Monterchi, local Italians gather to pay their respects at the three memorials in the town, one of them is British. We, along with many other British expatriates and members of the Royal British Legion would be among those that gathered. This was to be a special ceremony as the

British Legion had brought hundreds of poppies for the Italians to wear in their lapels as a symbol of unity and friendship.

*

As December began to bring the year to a close we received an urgent message from one of our neighbours that not all of their olive harvest had been gathered in. The weather was changing and what remained on the trees was in danger of perishing. Olive farmers know exactly when to harvest, the ideal time often varies according to the weather conditions from early autumn through into December. It also depends on the area and the extent of ripeness that the farmer wants from his crop. Some olives are picked when they are still green to preserve in jars, whilst others are left until they are a reddish purple colour. Although still unripe these

285

olives are more nutritious and once pressed will produce higher quality flavoured oil. The nets come out, the ladders go up and the land fills with agricultural workers, their families and helpers. The roads are crammed with tractors and trailers of all shapes and sizes; three wheeled open backed Apes stacked high with baskets, empty crates and harvesting nets are left as if abandoned by roadsides and gateways in readiness.

The nets are laid out around the base of the trees and pegged with small wooden stakes to keep them in place, they are to catch the falling fruit that the tree climbers shake, pick or comb from the branches.

In some parts of Tuscany the harvesters are paid in olive oil rather than cash, undeclared and undetected by the fiscal authorities. An experienced olive picker can harvest up to ninety kilos in a day and depending on how much oil the olives yield, the gatherer can receive around five litres of oil a day for their work. Many of the older olive pickers still use apron shaped baskets. The baskets are made from small branches; they are flat on one side and curved in a semi-circular bowl shape on the other. The flat side is held in place by a belt and positioned against the picker's stomach whilst the curve to the front acts as a pouch, leaving their hands free to collect the olives.

Our friends Freya and Malcolm needed helpers so we rallied to their cause. It was a dry day albeit a bit damp and overcast, the low cloud still clinging to the tops of the mountains, the sun desperately trying to burn through. When we arrived the harvest was in full swing. The majority of their sixty-four trees had already been stripped and what was left would need to be picked that day. Pamela was there, as well as Chris with our four legged friend Seamus who sat ears pricked and tail wagging, intrigued by the urgent activity that was going on around him, a well tethered lead was all that prevented him from joining in.

The olives came away from the long feathery branches with relative ease, some plucked by hand, the others simply falling from the branches as they were shaken, a rake like claw took care of the most stubborn fruit and after four hours of bending, stooping and stretching all the olives lay in the nets. The next stage was to transfer the olives into the crates and carry them to the drying floor in the barn. Any leaves or bits of twig were removed. Freya had devised a method of extracting most of the moisture on the skins of the olives by rolling them around in an old duvet cover; they were then laid out to dry naturally on the floor of the barn.

After a few days and back in the crates the olives were taken to the *frantoio* at Anghiari for pressing. Here they were put through a washer to remove any final impurities before being crushed whole, stones included, using a variety of granite millstones. The olive paste that is produced is then layered onto mats called *fiscoli*, which are stacked high with a metal discs inserted in between each layer. These are then subjected to pressure from a hydraulic press or screw. The liquid that is produced drains through the mats and is collected ready for the final separation process. The liquid now just oil and water is introduced to a centrifugal separator, which eliminates the water together with any impurities, once completed the oil is then ready for bottling.

The olive trees produced four hundred and eight kilos of olives, which in turn produced seventy-two litres of wonderful extra virgin oil, which is full of flavour and has a pepperiness that makes your tongue tingle. For me personally, there is no better way to appreciate the fresh pungent buttery taste of the oil, than to simply enjoy it with fresh bread or drizzled over a green salad.

# CHAPTER 19

It was Christmas and the wood that we had cut would last us well into the New Year. Over the next few days I would have plenty of time to reflect on the journey that had brought Nick and I to this secluded Chestnut Barn in Tuscany. The Barn was warm and I could stare happily into the glow from the wood-burner and let my thoughts run. The flashing delicate white lights on the tree reflected on the large un-curtained windows that looked out onto the wild winter scene beyond. I thought of old friends and family whose cards of seasonal good wishes hung on strings from the chestnut beams, we would miss them.

It had not been easy, there had been trials and tribulations that neither of us would have expected but we were still here. My Italian has improved and Nicks is still almost non-existent, then I thought of the time back in England when we had enthusiastically embarked with two other friends on an Italian language course at the local college. A group of about thirty people of various ages had also enrolled and I wondered, why Italian? Did they too have a secret to tell, a dream of another life? Nick had initially taken to the learning process quite well and went along each week without any persuasion from me, but I fear it was the two or three pints at the pub afterwards that was the main attraction for him. After three weeks of lectures and homework we were almost getting to the conversational stage and then it happened. We were to be paired off with total strangers with a view to conversation, in other words Italian role-plays. We were each given a scenario and were about to be told to go off with our newly selected partners to the side of the room and begin acting out our roles. I was partnered with what I believed to be a 40 year old male hairdresser who wore leather trousers, had bleached blonde hair and a fake tan. For Nick our lecturer had chosen a large, plump, elderly lady with a beaming smile, who kept nodding across at him, eager it seemed to get things moving, she put me in mind of Margaret Rutherford.

"I'm not doing it." I heard him say discretely at first from the side of his mouth, the plump elderly lady still smiling had left her seat and was heading towards him.

"I'm bloody well not doing it."
The words, louder this time had turned heads around the room. And with that he was off and running, the chair he was sitting on crashed to the floor and 29 gaping mouths followed him towards the door; our lecturer was still talking while writing something on the blackboard. When the door slammed behind him he had gained the attention of all-present.

"Not feeling too well I think." I offered, and that was that. After the session my friends and I found him chatting away to some stranger in the pub as if nothing had happened. Happy it seems to have a conversation with somebody he didn't know in English. When we questioned him he said,

"I'm not into 'Amdram' and I'm sure as hell not doing it with a stranger in my own time."

And there the lessons ended, for Nick anyway. I decided to pay for private lessons with the same tutor, who came to our house and I had to make excuses for his absence while he secretly hid himself away upstairs. I hoped that the noise of the creaking floorboards as he tiptoed around wouldn't give him away.

I laughed out loud in the glow of the fire, it would be an evening of my quiet private chuckles and questioning glances over the cover of the Christmas present he was reading.

I looked at the pile of neatly cut logs in buckets beside the fire, logs that had been cut during several days of blood, sweat and almost tears. We gone to the forest to attack the biggest dead chestnut tree we had, enough wood he said optimistically "to last the winter." The trunk was wider than the whole length of the chainsaw blade; the height was at least fifty feet. To cut it down he had to make several cuts around the tree ending with a wedge facing the direction he wanted it to fall. After an hour a loud crack could be heard and I could see him preparing to run for safety, but suddenly the tree slumped on one side, the wrong side; the blade of the saw was crushed and trapped in the tree. He went for the axe in the hope of freeing the blade by cutting away wedges and he worked on the tree for another hour. Eventually he managed to detach the chainsaw engine from the oval shaped runner the chain ran along and gradually manoeuvred the runner free using the axe as a wedge, the chain stayed firmly where it was. He went for another chain and eventually the chainsaw running again. After cutting another deeper wedge he used the axe as a lever to try and move the tree but the axe handle snapped leaving the head firmly embedded in the trunk. Eventually the tree began its fall, initially in the planned direction but suddenly it rotated away to the left and lodged itself against an oak tree. The angle of the trunk was no more than a few degrees. At that he gave up for the day but the worrying angle of the massive trunk as it leaned over the track made for a sleepless night.

"It could kill Florio if he comes up on Monday; it has to come down before then."

Three days later it was a pile of logs. I giggled again at the thought of what he termed as unnatural 'conspiracies' through no fault of his own; a job that should have taken hours had turned into a labour lasting several days. He would say,

"You start one job and end up with four."

"And when you break something" referring to the axe, "you never know where to get it repaired."

There were many such uphill struggles in this first year, most he could cope with but the bureaucracy was something else. It could be the one thing that could bring my dream to an end.

When we returned to England Nick had brought with him one of his most treasured possessions, a cased antique percussion pistol dating from around 1850. It was a piece of artistry all of its own with scrolled carvings on all of the metal parts. A gunsmith who was born in the same village as he was had made it so it had sentimental value. It couldn't be fired unless you possessed black powder and ball; in England you could own such a collectors item without a firearms licence. Before bringing the gun to Italy Nick had made enquiries of a gun dealer he knew in London who confirmed that under European law it was considered a 'curiosity', a collectible antique for which a licence was not required. On the strength of this expert advice Nick decided to buy another similar pistol, but this time a Scottish pistol from an Italian auctioneer based in Sarzana near Pisa. He planned to start building another collection and after making a successful bid on their online auction site he telephoned the auctioneer and asked if he could come and collect it in person, a nice day out we thought. But Oh No! A bureaucratic nightmare was unleashed in the space of the sixty-second telephone conversation.

'That's fine no problem' the auctioneer replied, 'just make sure you bring your Italian firearms licence with you when you come.'

"Uh, excuse me, I don't need a licence do I?" Nick responded.

"In Italy indeed you do, the laws are very strict and the penalties for possession of an illegal firearm are very severe, I'll wait to hear from you' she said and the call ended.

Not only had Nick purchased a firearm illegally but now he was also in possession of one that he had inadvertently brought into the country, on top of that had brought it through French territory without permission from the customs authorities.

Immediate retrospective action was required in order to correct an oversight that could have far reaching consequences.

A visit to the local police at the *comune* offices with a photograph of the pistol that the auctioneer had agreed to keep safe for Nick, brought the response

"We think it's alright because it's an antique but you need to check with the *Carabinieri*, I'll give them a ring. After the telephone conversation ended we were told that the local Commandant needed to see the photograph immediately so off we went. The response was similar, "We think it's alright but you'll need to speak to the *Polizia di Stato* in Sansepolcro."

Three days later we stood before a sergeant in a gleaming blue uniform who advised us that we needed to go to the *Questura* the police headquarters based in Arezzo.

Several days had now passed but following a chance meeting with the commandant of the *Carabinieri* we explained what had happened and he kindly agreed to look into it. In Italy these things take time but when we hadn't heard for over a week we went in pursuit of the commandant again. In the local commando centre I was offered a chair while the commandant made a series of telephone calls one of them to the auctioneer, I think to make sure the gun was actually there and not already in our possession, we hadn't mentioned the well travelled 'you know what' that was already here. The decision was made; Nick had to have an Italian licence to carry firearms. The commandant provided Nick with a list of things he had to do before he would be granted his licence.

First stop was to see our doctor to obtain a certificate stating that Nick was of sound mind. Now our doctor has known us since Nick's accident and hospitalisation but only for a relatively short time no more than two years, nevertheless the certificate was immediately forthcoming for the private fee of twelve euros. Next we had to make an appointment in Sansepolcro to see an eye specialist for the regulatory eye test and on payment of fifty-six euros the test was arranged for the following week.

At the hospital two senior doctors examined Nicks eyes one entered details on a computer while the other carried out the test. Having removed his glasses he had to read the usual series of letters from the top down which was fine until the smaller letters midway down began to suggest speculation rather than accuracy. From where I was standing I could see the mistakes but the doctor just said '*Sì Sì, va bene, perfetto*' and gave him a score of 8 out of 10, whilst the other doctor asked him why he needed glasses at all!

With most of the relevant certificates of proficiency already gathered we had to make a visit to the local rifle range where Nick would have to prove his ability at handling a gun. Now this *was* an experience, we waited for three hours whilst various officers of the law carried out their annual competency tests, firing automatic hand pistols at targets in the shape of human torsos. The sound was almost deafening. Next it was Nick's turn, he was led in a nervous state to the firing range having been issued with a set of ear defenders and a clip of fifty rounds of ammunition that he had to hand to the examiner on arrival. Most of the weapons fired were officially issued Glock automatics, which never seemed to run out of ammunition. Nick was to fire an automatic rifle at a target fifty metres away. A large man with muscles upon muscles took the clip from Nick; I imagine he needed to test the rifle first. After firing round after round he handed the rifle to Nick with brief instructions, mainly in sign language of what he had to do next.

"You must place the sight in the centre of the circle at the end of the barrel and line it up with the target down there," pointing to what Nick described as a blur of a white dot. With 'varifocal' glasses it is extremely difficult to combine long and short distances and Nick could see the end of the rifle through the bottom of his lenses but the target was a total wipe out, if he focussed on the target with the top of the lens he couldn't see the gun sight at all. He ended up by having to guess. Bullets went everywhere and dust was spurting up from a mound of earth behind the white dot, and the burly man could barely contain himself. I sat in the office with the President who would be making the final decision based on the questions I had answered and on the evidence provided by the target and the examiner. Finally they both arrived.

"*Signora*" he said pointing to the centre of the target that had been completely annihilated "Your husband is a good shot, this not so good" he said, pointing to a ring of holes that were completely wide of the centre. So four hours later and another one hundred and ten euros lighter, we emerged. With all the papers now in place we returned to the *Polizia di Stato* and two weeks later my gentle husband who wouldn't hurt a fly became licensed to kill!

I had to ask how he felt about all the rings we had had to jump through for a little piece of history; he just laughed and said "funny wasn't it." For the first time during our year spent here I had a real sense of feeling that there would be no going back...

Printed in Great Britain
by Amazon

35969685R00180